Again the Israelites did evil in the eyes of the LORD, now that Ehud was dead. So the LORD sold them into the hands of Jabin king of Canaan, who reigned in Hazor. Sisera, the commander of his army, was based in Harosheth Haggoyim. Because he had nine hundred chariots fitted with iron and had cruelly oppressed the Israelites for twenty years, they cried to the LORD for help.

Now Deborah, a prophet, the wife of Lappidoth, was leading Israel at that time.

—Judges 4:1–4 (NIV)

Extraordinary Women OF THE BIBLE

Extraordinary Women OF THE BIBLE

THE WOMAN WARRIOR

DEBORAH'S STORY

Virginia Smith

Guideposts

Extraordinary Women OF THE BIBLE

THE WOMAN WARRIOR

DEBORAH'S STORY

ACKNOWLEDGMENTS

I would like to acknowledge my mother, Amy Barkman, who is a Bible scholar and a writer in her own right. She patiently listened to me describe story ideas and possibilities, and offered suggestions that found their way into this book. I'm also extremely grateful for the awesome editorial team at Guideposts. Their attention to detail and their love for biblical fiction made this story better. I don't want to forget to mention my long-suffering husband, who kept the household running and put up with countless lonely hours while I was upstairs in my office, pounding away at the keyboard.

But most of all, I am grateful to Yahweh. Every good story comes from Him.

Cast of
CHARACTERS

Adena • daughter of Dara and Chaim; betrothed to Tivon

Amos • archer in the Israeli army

Amram • Israelite from Judah

Anna • newcomer to the village; woman who seeks Deborah's wisdom; wife of Levi

Asif • villager; does not approve of Deborah "pretending" to hear from God or of her teaching men

Barak • commander of Israel's army

Benjamin • villager; Reuben's younger brother

Chaim • farmer; Adena's father; his land lies at the northern border of Lappidoth's and Deborah's

Dara • farmer; Adena's mother; Deborah's friend

Daniel • villager; Elana's husband

Deborah • a woman who lives in Ephraim; Israel's fourth judge, and only woman judge

Ehud • Israel's second prophet and judge

Elana • villager; wife of Daniel

Eliakim • Benjamite; joins Israelite army

Elias • farmer; brother of Uri

Elinat • villager

Elizabeth • villager; Dara's sister

Gersham • farmer; Uri's father

Haran • villager; son of Tima

Heber • Kenite; Jael's husband

Jabin • Canaanite king

Jael • Kenite; Heber's wife

Joel • farmer; son of Tima

Laban • son of Dara and Chaim

Lappidoth • farmer; Deborah's husband

Leah • villager; makes and sells jewelry

Levi • newcomer to the village; Anna's husband

Lilah • Uri's deceased mother

Malka • villager; Reuben's mother and Ophira's daughter-in-law

Oded • Benjamite; joins Israelite army

Ophira • villager; woman who seeks Deborah's wisdom; wife of
  Reuben

Othniel • Israel's first judge

Phineas • Israeli military leader under Barak

Rachel • villager; woman who comes to Deborah's teaching; Seth's
  wife

Reuben • villager; potter; Ophira's husband

Sabra • Deborah's daughter

Samuel • villager; wool merchant

Seth • villager; Rachael's husband

Shamgar • Israel's third judge

Shira • villager; Rachel's mother

Sisera • commander of the Canaanite army

Tima • villager; woman who seeks Deborah's wisdom

Tivon • son of Deborah and Lappidoth; betrothed to Adena

Tyrek • newcomer to the village; brother of Ophira

Uri • farmer; son of Gersham

Yadon • farmer

Yocheved • Deborah's aunt

Yosef • villager; Reuben's father; a potter

Zeb • farmer; Uri's brother

Glossary of TERMS

abba • father

Aseret Ha'devarim • the Ten Declarations (or Commandments)

Bereshith • the book of Genesis; the first book of Torah

BaMidbar • the book of Numbers; the fourth book of Torah

imma • mother

doda • aunt

Elohim • God

gerah • a unit of currency, equal to 1/20th of a sacred shekel (Numbers 18:16)

gerim • foreigners

mattan • gifts a man gives to his bride when they marry; this is different from the *mohar*, which is given to the bride's father

mitzvah • commandment

mohar • the bride price; a bridegroom paid this to the father of his intended wife

Richan • Sunday, the first day of the Israeli's week

senet • a board game from ancient Egypt

Shabbat • Israel's day of rest

shalom • peace; a deeper meaning is wholeness, oneness with God

Shavuot • the Jewish Feast of Weeks; it is exactly seven weeks after the second day of Passover; in the book of Acts, the Holy Spirit came upon the disciples on Shavuot, which Christians call Pentecost

tannur • a portable clay oven or stove

Torah • Israel's holy books; the first five books of the Christian Old Testament

Vayikra • the book of Leviticus; the third book of Torah

CHAPTER ONE

The sun beat down on the baked clay roof and rendered the air inside Deborah's house sweltering and nearly unbreathable. She knelt before the quern and applied the millstone to a handful of grain, singing in a low voice and doing her best to ignore the sweat trickling its way down her face. Her daughter, Sabra, sat in the doorway, hoping to catch a stray breeze, and applied a needle to patch a section of ripped fabric. Such heat was unusual so early in the year, as if the earth itself joined in the laments of Yahweh's people. She fervently hoped the earth's weather would resume its normal pattern soon.

"I do not see why I must mend Tivon's tunic when he will only rip it again." A whine of complaint saturated Sabra's voice, a tone that Deborah had noticed all too often of late.

She stopped singing and answered with a laugh in her voice. "You would have him work the fields without benefit of clothing?"

"I would have him take greater care," the girl replied. "And perhaps show a bit of gratitude." She pulled a stitch tight. "Perhaps if he had to mend his own tunic, he would be more appreciative."

Deborah did not answer. Sabra's thirteenth birthday drew near, and it seemed every day she grew more impatient with

1

her brother. And with her mother, truth be told. *Yahweh, she is nearly grown. Only You know what her future holds. Bless her with a happy life.*

Her daughter's life had been laid out since shortly after her birth. She was to marry a cousin, the eldest son of Lappidoth's brother in Shechem. Three years past, Shechem was attacked by a band of Canaanites, and the boy was killed along with many others. The tragedy had devastated them all.

The grain on the quern had become a fine powder beneath her stone. She swept it into a jar and reached for another handful of grain.

Sabra stood abruptly. "We have a visitor." Excitement colored her tone. She tossed her brother's tunic aside and hurried toward the storage room, announcing as she went, "I will bring a cool drink to refresh her."

Deborah didn't bother to hide a knowing smile. A visitor meant a break in routine, something her daughter relished. Anything to take her away from chores she found tedious.

A woman appeared in the open doorway and peered inside. "Deborah?"

"Ophira." Deborah sat back on her heels. "Come inside."

The woman entered and lowered her head covering to her shoulders. "I do not wish to interrupt."

"Join me." Deborah waved her over. "We can talk while I work."

If she stopped work for every visitor, nothing would ever get done. It had begun with one woman from a neighboring farm coming to Deborah for advice. Before she knew what had happened, her reputation in the village as a wise woman spread. Even older women came to seek her guidance. Deborah never failed to acknowledge the Source of her wisdom or to give thanks to Yahweh for each woman He allowed her to help.

Ophira left her shoes by the door and settled on a woven mat near the quern. Deborah retrieved the millstone and again began to methodically reduce the grain to powder. Ophira watched silently. From the corner of her eye Deborah noted the younger woman's tense shoulders and tightly drawn features.

Yahweh, something disturbs her. Help me put her at ease.

A question fell from her lips almost without thought. "Have you had word from your *abba*?"

She was not surprised when the young woman drew in a quick breath. "How did y—"

Her words stopped when Sabra appeared from the storage room carrying a tray. She crossed the distance slowly and set the tray on the floor opposite Deborah, then lowered herself to another mat.

"I've brought water to cool you from the heat."

She handed a mug to Ophira, who took it with a smile of thanks. The smile dissolved a moment later, the woman's gaze sliding to Deborah.

"Thank you, daughter," Deborah said, accepting her own mug.

Taking the third mug from the tray, Sabra settled herself comfortably and then fixed a gaze on Ophira. "Is your husband well?"

Ophira had recently married the eldest son of a potter in the village. She sipped from her mug, then gave a quick nod. "Reuben is well."

"And his *imma*?" Sabra asked. "Have you settled into a peaceful routine?"

"We work well together."

Deborah watched her daughter attempt to draw their guest into polite conversation. Could she not see Ophira's discomfort? Was it not obvious that she wanted to speak privately with Deborah?

"Sabra, I believe the goats need tending," Deborah said. "Would you see that they have food and fresh water?"

Resentment flashed onto her young features. Her chest inflated with a quick breath, but Deborah spoke again before she could voice an argument.

"The heat is fierce today, and there isn't much shade for the poor things." She held Sabra's gaze and arched her eyebrows in a silent command.

Sabra understood. Her chest deflated with a breath blown through her nose that was almost, but not quite, a frustrated snort.

"Yes, Imma."

She set her mug on the tray and rose. With a quick nod at Ophira, she left the house. Moments later they heard her singsong voice drifting through the open door from the direction of the courtyard where they housed their animals.

"She's nearly grown," Deborah told her visitor, "and wants badly to be thought of as such."

Ophira gave a distracted nod, her expression still pinched. She gulped from the mug and then clutched it in her lap with both hands. "Why did you ask if I have heard from my abba?"

Deborah pondered her answer. Finally, she admitted, "I do not know. The question came to mind and felt right to ask."

She might have gone on to explain that Yahweh's wisdom often came to her like that, as a thought that did not feel like her own, or an urge to speak words without pausing to wonder why.

"I received a scroll from Jericho. Asif read it to me for two coins."

Deborah kept her expression blank. Asif, whose family ran the village's only olive press, served as a scribe for those not fortunate enough to have been taught to read or write. Though he had been taught by priests and was widely regarded as wise, Deborah found him to be a harsh man. He never failed to find fault with the beeswax wicks she fashioned and supplied for the lamps in the Tabernacle in Shiloh.

"I hope all is well in Jericho," she said.

"It is. That is to say, Abba did not say otherwise." Her head drooped forward.

Deborah prompted her to continue. "Your abba had a request for you?"

Ophira looked up then, misery in the eyes that fixed on Deborah. "He wants to send my brother here, to be apprenticed along with my husband as a potter."

It was unusual for a man, even a father, to make such a request of his daughter. The letter should have been sent to Yosef himself, the potter.

"Have you relayed the request to Yosef?" she asked.

Ophira shook her head. "I have not told Reuben either," she added, clearly miserable.

Was she afraid of her husband and of his abba? No, that did not feel right. But if not, then what troubled the young woman? *Yahweh?*

The answer came as clearly as spring water.

"Tell me about your brother."

Words poured from Ophira's lips then, as if a dam had broken. "Tyrek is wild. Even as a child he caused more mischief than anyone else in Jericho. The teachers of the Law cast him out, saying he caused disruption among the young men. Abba gave him watch over our sheep with instructions to take them into the hillside, thinking lonely nights would tame him. But he took a wineskin and drank it dry and fell asleep." She leaped to her feet and began to pace. "A wolf attacked and killed a ewe who was near to birthing a lamb. The rest of the flock scattered. Tyrek left with fifteen and returned with four."

Deborah shut her eyes against a flood of sympathy. Such a loss could devastate a family.

Ophira's pacing quickened. She reached the back window, whirled, and returned. "Then Abba set him to tending the wheat field. But Tyrek said the work did not suit him. Instead, he left Jericho to become a fisherman." She stopped beside Deborah. "That was before my marriage to Reuben. Abba's message said Tyrek has returned, claiming that fishing was not to his liking."

"And now your abba wishes to send him to Yosef to see if he can become a potter."

"Yosef is a kind man." Ophira's eyes filled with tears. "He will welcome my brother if I ask. But Tyrek will cause trouble, as he always does." She dropped cross-legged onto the mat and buried her face in her hands. "Tyrek has no regard for Yahweh. He will bring strife into the household."

Deborah rose to her knees, picked up her millstone, and began grinding the grain.

Yahweh, Ophira is right. This young man will disrupt the peace of not only Yosef's household but of the entire village. There are already too many of Your children who have turned away from You here. One more, and a mischief-maker at that, will cause even more disorder.

The familiar sounds of the stone crushing grain filled her ears. A gentle comfort settled in her soul. Without words, even without thought, Deborah knew Yahweh's answer.

"Do you know the words of the covenant Yahweh gave to Moses, the *Aseret Ha'devarim* that are carved into the stone tablets in the Tabernacle in Shiloh?"

The young woman lifted her face. "Yes, I do."

"Of those ten *mitzvah*, only one comes with a promise. Do you know which that is?"

Ophira's eyes became distant with thought. Deborah continued her work with the stone.

"Honor your father and your mother, that your days may be long in the land that Yahweh is giving you."

Deborah nodded. "You cannot compel your brother to change his attitude or his actions, and Yahweh does not expect that of you. But He does expect you to obey Him."

"But what if Tyrek becomes a burden to my husband's family?"

Deborah allowed a smile. "Oh, he will. For a while. But Yahweh has plans for Tyrek, plans that can only come to fruition if he is here. Not in Jericho."

Ophira tilted her head, her features filled with skepticism. "How do you know?"

A chuckle rumbled through Deborah's chest. "Because Yahweh knows. You came for advice, and here it is. When you honor your abba by relaying his request, tell your husband and Yosef what you have told me. The decision will be theirs. And then commit your brother to Yahweh's care."

Ophira shook her head. "Tyrek does not know Yahweh."

"But Yahweh knows him. And you. You can trust Yahweh."

"Thank you." For the first time since her arrival, Ophira's features relaxed. "What can I do for you in return for your advice?"

Deborah laughed. "Give your praise to Yahweh, the Source of all wisdom."

The young woman rose and went to the doorway to slip on her sandals. She pulled her head covering up over her head.

"One more thing," Deborah said, and Ophira turned. "If you receive further messages, I will gladly read them for you and take no coin in return."

With a final grateful smile, Ophira left.

———————

The afternoon brought no respite from the heat. Deborah sent Sabra to start a fire with kindling and dung in the outdoor *tannur* while she mixed dough for the evening's bread. After twenty years of marriage to Lappidoth and keeping his house, the task was so familiar she barely paid attention to the work of her hands. Her thoughts drifted to a passage from *Torah*, from Yahweh's instruction to Moses in urging Pharoah to release His people from enslavement. And the river shall bring forth frogs abundantly, which shall go up and come into thine house, and into thy bedchamber, and upon thy bed, and into the house of thy servants, and upon thy people, and into thine ovens, and into thy kneading troughs. A chuckle rumbled in her throat as it always did when she thought of that passage. How startled Egyptian housewives must have been while performing this same task that occupied Deborah now, only to have a plague of frogs leap into their bowls.

"Imma." Deborah looked up to find Sabra standing in the doorway. "We have visitors."

The girl wore an oddly hesitant expression.

Deborah continued to mix the warm dough. "Show them in."

"But—"

A woman pushed past her. "Deborah, I need you to settle an argument."

"Tima." Deborah forced a smile of welcome, though truth be told, she had always found the woman to be harsh and not a little difficult. "You've caught me in the middle—"

She fell silent when Tima gestured for two more people to enter. Her sons. No wonder Sabra hesitated to admit them. It was considered unseemly for a woman to entertain a man in her home in her husband's absence.

After patting the dough into a ball in the kneading trough, she rubbed her hands together to dislodge the residue. "Perhaps we should go outside. Sabra, would you finish for me?"

She started to rise, but Tima jerked an impatient gesture in her direction. "There is no reason for that. This will only take a moment." Her eyes narrowed and she cast a meaningful look at Sabra. "It is a *private* matter."

Sabra's gaze slid to Deborah, who gave a tiny nod. Turning with a huff, she stomped out of the house.

Tima stared after her. "You had best get a handle on that girl, Deborah. Before you turn around twice she will be an unruly wench, and then what will you do?"

With an effort, Deborah maintained a calm demeanor. "Thank you for your advice, Tima."

The woman preened, obviously pleased that her warning had been received as advice by the one famous for giving advice.

Deborah glanced at the two young men, who both managed to look flustered. Though she should insist on exiting the house, these two were Tima's sons. Surely no one would call her to task for entertaining them and their mother in her home.

"Haran." She nodded at the first, who shifted his weight from one foot to the other. "Joel." The younger dropped his head and did not meet her gaze. She looked again at Tima. "What help can I provide?"

"You can instruct my youngest son as to the care of his widowed mother." Tima's jaw jutted forward.

Deborah glanced at Joel, who had not raised his head.

Haran took a half step forward. "My brother insists on leaving half of our harvest lying on the field to be picked up by *Gentiles*." He spat the last word.

"By *Gentiles*," Tima repeated, mimicking her oldest son's tone.

Scripture filtered through Deborah's mind. Lessons from Torah she had been privileged to learn as a young person, to memorize and hold close in her heart. Still, she held her tongue.

"Joel!" His mother snapped the name. "Tell her."

The young man's head dipped lower. "There is a Moabite woman."

"Moabite!" Tima shrieked the word. "A Moabite, Deborah. A Gentile of the worst kind."

Deborah did not take her eyes from the young man. "Go on, please."

Joel's chest inflated. "She is a widow."

"*I* am a widow!" Tima screeched.

The young man winced. "She is a widow without means of provision. She has no property, no family. And she reveres Yahweh. Her husband was Hebrew and died in a skirmish with the Canaanites." The young man lifted his head to lock Deborah's gaze. "If we do not help her, she will die."

"He lusts after her." Haran turned his head and spat upon the packed-dirt floor.

Deborah would have admonished him, but she held her tongue. Yahweh's wisdom had begun to stir her soul. The Lord her God had a word to share, though at this point she knew not what it might be.

"Not so." Joel's head shot upright, anger plain in his voice. "I have compassion for her. Does not Yahweh urge us to have compassion for the less fortunate?"

"*I* am the less fortunate." Tima beat a fist upon her breast. "Am I not a widow dependent on the kindness of my family?"

Deborah had to lower her own head, to hide a secret smile. Joel spoke Yahweh's heart. But how to phrase the judgment so Tima and Haran could accept it?

She closed her eyes. *Yahweh, what is Your judgment here? Give me Your wisdom.*

After a long moment, she looked up at Joel. "Are you giving this widow more than her share?" She paused and held his gaze for a long moment. "Are you leaving more than a tithe's portion for her to glean?"

His eyelids fluttered down, and he again lowered his head. "Perhaps I am."

A song erupted in Deborah's soul. In an instant she *knew*. It was as though Yahweh allowed her a brief glimpse into Joel's soul. A wave of compassion washed over her at the tenderness she found in the young man's heart.

"You see?" Tima glared at her youngest. "He forces his imma to go without while feeding the mouth of a pagan Moabite."

A question rose up in Deborah's spirit. "Are you truly without, Tima? Are you starving? Do your sons not care for their widowed mother?"

In the face of such a direct question, Tima let her shoulders droop. Her glance slid toward Haran before she answered, "My sons are dutiful. I am not in want."

Lord, let Your wisdom shine through me.

Deborah smiled, trusting that she had opened herself up to Yahweh's wisdom for this situation. She straightened to her full height, which attained the height of neither of the men before her. "Do you know what Torah says regarding widows?"

Joel's head shot upward. "It says we should take care of widows, and also that we should allow widows to glean from the fields." His head lowered for a moment. "Honestly I do not know where that passage is, but I know it is there."

Tima took steps toward him. "I am a widow, my son. Would you put that harlot on the same level as me?"

The struggle on the young man's face wrenched in Deborah's stomach.

"No, Imma," he whispered. "But she is not a harlot. She is merely hungry."

A passage from Torah rose in Deborah's mind. She could not stop her smile. Joel was right. She paused a moment, in which her kinship with the younger son grew, and she warmed to his cause.

"Joel is correct," she announced. She poured the authority given her by Yahweh into her voice, and the Lord her God answered by pouring power through her words. "Yahweh says: 'You shall not ill-treat any widow or orphan. If you do mistreat them, I will heed their outcry as soon as they cry out to Me, and My anger shall blaze forth and I will put you to the sword, and your own wives shall become widows and your children orphans.'"

She paused to let that sink in. The color drained from Haran's ruddy cheeks. He had taken a wife a few years ago, and the couple recently welcomed their second child.

Watching Tima's face, she continued. "Elsewhere Yahweh instructs: 'When thou cuttest down thine harvest in thy field, and hast forgot a sheaf in the field, thou shalt not go again to fetch it: it shall be for the stranger, for the fatherless, and for the widow: that the Lord thy God may bless thee in all the work of thine hands.'" She caught and held Tima's gaze. "Yahweh does not differentiate between an Israelite widow and a Gentile widow. If you are not in need, perhaps you should rejoice that your son has found a way to bless a Gentile and thus exemplify the power of Yahweh."

"She is a *Moabite*!" Tima said. "Does Torah not also say that we must destroy the foreigners who dwell in the land Yahweh promised our forefathers?"

Deborah struggled to maintain a calm expression, for she knew full well that Tima had not joined the rest of the villages in the pilgrimage feasts to the tabernacle in Shiloh. It was whispered that she had even been observed offering sacrifices to Baal.

"As our ancestors claimed our birthright, yes. But we dare not forget that we were foreigners in Egypt. We must always remember. Yahweh also commands, 'You shall not oppress a stranger, for you know the feelings of the stranger, having yourselves been gerim in the land of Egypt.'"

"But that—that is—" Tima's lips clamped shut into a hard line.

Deborah softened her tone. "It is a hard teaching, I know."

Haran spoke up then. "But the one passage contradicts the other." He threw his hands into the air. "How are we to understand the will of Yahweh in the face of such inconsistency?"

After a long moment, during which Deborah sought Yahweh's answer, she nodded. "I confess I struggle to understand as well. Until I remember that Yahweh loves the fatherless and the widow and gives them food and clothing. Are we to do less?"

"This is worthless." Tima threw her hands into the air. "How can we follow the teaching of a God who asks us to take food from our children's mouths and give it to harlots?" She whirled and stomped out of the house.

Haran hesitated, his gaze fixed on Deborah as though testing her. After a long moment, he followed his imma, leaving Deborah alone with Joel.

"Thank you," the young man said. "I am sorry for the trouble my family has caused this day."

He started to turn away, but Deborah stopped him. "There is another teaching in Torah concerning the foreigners among us that I would have you consider."

Caution stole over his expression. He nodded for her to continue.

"'You shall not intermarry with them.'" She watched him flinch. "'You shall not give your daughter to his son, and you shall not take his daughter for your son. For they will turn away your son from following Me, and they will worship the gods of others, and the wrath of the Lord will be kindled against you, and He will quickly destroy you.'"

He shook his head in protest. "I will not turn away from the God of my fathers."

How clearly this young man's heart showed upon his face. Even in his protest, he admitted the feelings Deborah had glimpsed in his heart. He loved this Moabite widow. And yet in Joel she discerned something she had not seen in his brother or his imma. Joel revered Yahweh. In a time when so many had forgotten the God of their fathers and turned to idols, such devotion was rare.

"I am sorry," she said. "We are a people set apart since our father Abraham's covenant. Our lives are to be committed to Yahweh." She poured as much compassion into her voice as she could manage. "It is not always easy to serve the King of the universe."

She wanted to close her eyes against the pain she saw in his. But after a moment, he gave a silent nod.

"My advice is this: continue to have compassion on the Moabite widow, but do not leave for her more than you should. Give your imma and your brother no cause to fault you." She ducked her head to catch his eye. "You may one day persuade them to strengthen their own devotion to Yahweh."

A snort, full of scorn, blasted from his nostrils. "We will sooner see manna from heaven covering the fields than witness either of them worshiping Yahweh in more than word."

Deborah grinned. "It has happened before."

That did elicit a slight smile from the young man. A motherly rush of fondness washed over her. He would make a fine husband one day. Maybe even for...

"Come," she told him. "Let us go outside. Have you met my daughter, Sabra?"

At the doorway Joel paused for Deborah to exit first. She did, stepping over the bricks that separated their home from the surrounding pen where their animals were housed. For a moment the sun dazzled her eyes, and she blinked. When her vision cleared, her gaze fell on a passerby, a man wearing a shawl of draped linen over an inner tunic. In a flash she recognized Asif.

His gaze slid from hers to a point behind her and then settled on Joel. His eyes narrowed, and a wave of palpable animosity rushed toward her. Before she could call a greeting, or an explanation, he jerked his face away and hurried down the packed-dirt path.

Deborah drew in a breath. She had just been seen leaving her house with a man. Never mind that the man was young enough to be her son. He was a man, and she had entertained him alone in her house.

She would hear more of this. Of that she was certain.

CHAPTER TWO

The evening meal was taken on the roof. Deborah had elicited Sabra's aid in erecting a canopy made of densely woven fabric to shield the family from the sun that hung low on the western horizon. Beneath it they had spread the thickly woven rug which held their meal and placed mats around it for seating. As they ate, Lappidoth and Tivon described the day's labor in the family's fields.

"The olive trees are covered in new blooms." Tivon dipped a piece of bread into the bowl of seasoned oil. "We will need to prune the excess or risk the harvest breaking the branches."

Lappidoth nodded his agreement. "In a month, perhaps two. Until then, there is plenty of work in the field. The barley is nearing harvest."

"May I help prune the olive trees?" Sabra watched her abba with a hopeful expression.

Lappidoth's gaze slid to Deborah's.

"Only what you can reach from the ground," Deborah said.

Sabra's shoulders slumped, and her head dropped forward so that her chin nearly touched her chest. A pang of regret jabbed at Deborah's heart. She took no pleasure in disappointing the girl. When she was small, Lappidoth would lift Sabra onto his shoulders so she could reach high into the branches to harvest olives or dates. Later, Tivon would hoist her into the tree so she could climb on sturdy branches and reach even higher. Now that she was nearing womanhood, such behavior would be unseemly.

Lappidoth dipped his bread into a bowl of golden honey and then let the excess of the thick, sweet nectar drip. "Perhaps if we place the wagon below the lowest branches you could stand upon it." He grasped his beard and held it out of the way while he brought the bread to his lips.

Sabra's face brightened. "Thank you, Abba."

She cast a quick sideways glance at Deborah. One corner of her mouth curved almost imperceptibly, giving her a smug look, which Deborah pretended not to see. While she reveled in the relationship between father and daughter, it pained her to be at odds with Sabra. Lately it seemed as if that was the case more often than not. Deborah understood. Though Sabra had not yet bled, womanhood was nearly upon her. Already she performed most household tasks almost as well as Deborah herself. She desired to be considered a woman full grown and yet chafed at the restrictions placed on her as a woman, especially as the junior woman in a household.

"Imma, do you have a jar of these to spare?"

Deborah eyed her son. Tivon held a honeyed fig before his lips. The honey came from her own hives, placed near the fig trees to give the bees access to the fragrant blooms. Her bees had been generous, and the family's storage room held more jars full of the sweet, thick liquid than they could easily eat in a year.

"I do," she told Tivon.

"May I take one as a gift for Adena's imma?"

Sabra rolled her eyes toward the overhead canopy, which drew a frown from her brother. Tivon's betrothal last fall provided another irritation for Sabra, though she usually held her tongue if not her eyes. Adena was a year older than Sabra. When Adena attained womanhood, when her monthly bleeding began, wedding plans would commence. Would Sabra be excited to be involved in the wedding, or would it be another cause for jealousy?

The sooner Lappidoth and Deborah found a suitable man to whom their daughter could be betrothed, the better.

"Certainly," Deborah answered. "Please present it to Dara with my good wishes."

"Thank you." Tivon got up from his mat, his expression eager.

Deborah turned to her daughter. "Will you please fetch the jar on the third shelf, the red one with the flower etching?"

For once Sabra did not protest. She rose in one smooth movement and headed toward the stairs with a graceful pace.

When her children had disappeared from view, Deborah leaned toward Lappidoth and spoke in a low voice.

"We must arrange a match for Sabra. She will bleed soon."

Wrinkles creased his brow, and he glanced in the direction of the stairs. "How do you know?"

Deborah sat back on her heels and studied her husband's face. Had he not noticed the changes in his daughter? The curve of her hips, the way her breasts had begun to swell beneath her tunic? And especially her recent irritability?

"I know," she said dryly. "Trust me."

He heaved a heavy sigh. "There are few to choose from." Sadness crept into his tone. "At least among those who have kept themselves pure from the idolatry that infects so many in Ephraim these days."

Deborah shared his sorrow. In the years since the death of the prophet and judge Ehud, the tribes of Israel had once again fallen away from Yahweh. In the tribe of Ephraim, those who obeyed the mitzvah of Moses had dwindled to less than half. Gatherings of the faithful were poorly attended. In her journeys to the tabernacle in Shiloh, she saw that Ephraim was not the only tribe that pagan worship had infected. Indeed, Yahweh's people had become splintered. They no longer came together as a chosen people, but each tribe clung to itself.

"We need a judge, one as strong as Ehud was." Deborah rose up on her knees and began to clear the mat, piling the bowls on the platter. "Surely Yahweh will raise one up soon."

Lappidoth snatched a piece of bread before she moved the plate. "There was Shamgar a few years back."

Shamgar had arisen from obscurity, loudly proclaiming his loyalty to Yahweh and his passion for Israel. If the news carried to Ephraim by the nomadic tribes was to be believed, Shamgar had defended the Hebrew people with nothing more than an oxgoad, a farmer's tool, and had killed six hundred Philistines who were oppressing his people. But after the heroic feat, Shamgar disappeared into the obscurity from which he had come.

"I thought he would be the one," Deborah agreed sadly.

She started to rise, to take the tray down into the house, but Lappidoth stopped her with a raised hand. "I must speak with you concerning a...difficult matter."

Deborah scanned her husband's unhappy face and sank back on her heels. "What is it?"

He plucked at a thread on his tunic and did not meet her eye. "I had a visitor in the barley field today."

From his actions, she knew the visitor must have brought a complaint against someone. One of the children? No, her husband would not avoid her gaze in that case. The visitor must have voiced a grievance about her.

Asif.

"Did the visitor come carrying a tale about me?"

A pained expression took his features. "Is it true that you entertained a man alone in our home today?"

Deborah set her jaw. "May I explain?"

He held out a hand, a gesture for her to continue.

"Tima brought her sons to the house to consult on a matter of the Law." She kept her voice even. "She and Haran are at odds with Joel, who is practicing Torah by leaving wheat in their field for a widow to glean."

"A widow?"

"A Moabite widow," she said. "I told them Yahweh did not differentiate between Hebrew widows and Moabite widows, that the Lord's will is to care for all widows and orphans, and that by leaving a little extra for the Moabite woman to glean, Joel is keeping Torah."

Lappidoth stroked his beard with a thumb and forefinger as he considered her words. "You say Tima brought her sons? She was here with them?"

Deborah drew a deep breath. "Not the entire time," she admitted. "When I quoted from Torah, she became irate. She fled, and Haran followed after her." Lappidoth opened his mouth to speak, and she hurried on before he could come to a conclusion. "I was left alone with Joel for the span of five sentences. No more." Remembering their private conversation, she felt confidence seep in. "I sensed his feelings for the woman, and Yahweh urged me to warn him about intermarrying with foreigners. That is all."

He released a pent-up breath. "I wish you had taken him outside to relay Yahweh's wisdom. It is unseemly, Deborah."

"I know." She bowed her head. "It happened so quickly."

Lappidoth rose and crossed over the rug with one long step. At her side, he lifted her chin and gazed deeply into her eyes. "I do not blame you, my love. I trust you with my life. But we must—"

She hushed him with a finger across his mouth. "I know. We, who are committed to Yahweh, must set an example. I understand, and I agree." She let a smile creep onto her lips and into her voice. "Am I forgiven, Husband?"

His arms came around her waist, and he pulled her toward him. "You are forgiven, Wife."

In the moment before their lips met, Deborah whispered a prayer in her heart. *Thank You, Yahweh, for this man.*

When he pulled away, he wore a thoughtful expression. "This Joel, was he open to teaching from Torah?"

She nodded. "He was. I feel certain the Lord our God has plans for that young man. He is true to Yahweh, even though his family has succumbed to idolatry."

"That is good." His eyebrows crept upward. "He is of marrying age?"

Deborah followed his thoughts easily, since she herself had entertained the same idea earlier. "He is, but now is not the time for him. When he has rid himself of feelings for the poor widow he is helping, perhaps then." She paused. "Can you imagine Tima's reaction if you approached with an offer now, after I sided against her today?"

Lappidoth laughed. "Truly, I am tempted to see it."

She slapped playfully at his shoulder, and he tightened his arms around her waist, pulling her closer. Their lips were a heartbeat apart when a shout from below interrupted.

"Abba! Imma!" Sabra's shrill tone rang with urgency. "Come quickly. Tivon is being attacked by Canaanites!"

CHAPTER THREE

D eborah and Lappidoth raced after Sabra toward the farm
of Chaim, father to Tivon's betrothed. Fear threatened to
choke her when she glimpsed smoke curling into the sky just
over a swell in the land. The acrid odor burned her nostrils.
She wasted no breath on words but maintained a constant
prayer in her mind.

*King of the universe, protect my son. Rise up on his behalf. Yahweh,
our enemies are Your enemies. Scatter them before us and let them do
no harm to Tivon.* Though a mother could certainly be excused
for asking protection for her son, she corrected her petition.
Or to any of Your people.

When they topped the rise, the source of the smoke came
into view. Flames licked at the edge of a neatly planted wheat
field. In the distance she spotted five men on horseback galloping away. One leaned forward on his horse's neck, holding
a torch with which he brushed the mature wheat heads, leaving a ribbon of fire in his wake.

Canaanite men.

Deborah's heart pounded in her chest, as much from anxiety
as from exertion. Wheat was Chaim's primary crop. He bar-
tered wheat for olives and dates and for any staples his family
did not grow themselves. If their wheat harvest was destroyed,

the family would be hard-pressed to feed themselves come winter.

Lappidoth cupped his hands around his mouth and shouted. "Sabra."

She turned, and Lappidoth stabbed a finger toward the burning field. She nodded and changed direction. With a piercing glance at Deborah, he followed.

Deborah understood his unspoken instruction. She gathered her skirts in one hand and pushed her legs to run faster toward the house, where a small knot of people had gathered. She arrived at the same time as four men approaching from the east. A glance identified Gersham and his sons, whose land bordered Chaim's.

"To the field," she shouted when she drew close enough to be heard.

Gersham's gaze flickered past her and then, lifting his ax above his head and shouting a battle cry, charged in that direction. His sons followed.

Deborah arrived at the house. In a glance she took in the splintered gate in the livestock pen. The door leading inside the dwelling dangled sideways, as if it had been kicked in. The sound of a woman's wailing filled the air. Had someone been killed? Her heart tightened in her chest. Tivon?

Yahweh, no!

She raced toward a cluster of people standing in a circle and pushed her way through.

Chaim lay on the ground, not moving, his head in Dara's lap. Deborah scanned his prone body. Blood seeped from a gash in his head and saturated his wife's skirt. Still seeping, which meant his heart still beat. Dara's youngest, a boy of eight or so, knelt beside her, tears streaking his cheeks.

Her chest heaving from her run, Deborah glanced around those circling the injured man.

"Tivon." In an instant she took note of his blood-smeared cheek and the sweat beading on his brow. "Are you hurt?"

He shook his head.

There was no time to feel relief. She pointed toward the house. "Gather rugs and mats. Anything that can be used to beat the flames."

His eyebrows twisted with confusion. Had he not yet noticed the burning wheat? "The field," she shouted, pointing behind him. "All of you. Leave Chaim to me. Save this family's field."

Adena, Tivon's betrothed, looked in that direction and then gasped. "I will get them."

She dashed toward the house while the rest of the bystanders—their closest neighbors, Deborah realized—ran toward the burning wheat. Tivon would have followed Adena, but Deborah grabbed his arm. The last thing they needed was a report that the two had been alone in the house together. Even in the midst of a crisis, tongues would carry the tale.

"Help your abba."

He cast a glance after Adena but then obeyed. Satisfied, Deborah dropped to her knees and studied the injured man's face. *"Leave Chaim to me,"* she had said, but in truth she was no physician.

Yahweh, please show me what to do.

An egg-sized lump swelled beneath the gash. Chaim had suffered a blow to the head, then, not a sword cut. Was that better? She wasn't sure, but at least his skull had not been punctured. A quick inspection revealed no additional wounds.

Adena exited the house at a run then, her arms draped with rugs and mats. With one agonized glance at her abba's prone body, she raced toward the burning field as quickly as her burden would allow. Following her progress, Deborah saw Sabra leave the fire and run toward her to help.

Dara's wailing had quieted, though she continued to sob while rocking back and forth.

"Dara," Deborah said gently, "we need water and clean cloths. Will you fetch them?"

The boy opened his mouth to speak, but Deborah hushed him with a glance and a nearly imperceptible shake of her head.

"Dara." She laid a hand on the woman's arm. "Will you fetch what we need to clean your husband's wound?"

Dara lifted her gaze from Chaim's face to Deborah's. The pain in her dark eyes was enough to halt the breath in Deborah's chest, but she schooled her expression.

Dara's sobs subsided enough for a reply. "Yes. I will."

With gentle movements, she slid sideways and laid Chaim's head on the soft grass. Then she leaped to her feet and hurried into the house.

The boy spoke in a quiet voice. "You wanted to give her a task. Something to do so she would stop weeping."

Deborah eyed the child. Perceptive for his age. "You are right. I gave her a task to distract her."

His gaze lowered to Chaim's bloodied head, and his features pinched with worry. "Will Abba die?"

Deborah wanted to evade the question. She put a hand beneath Chaim's head and, ignoring the blood that had begun to congeal in his hair, turned his face so she could better see the wound. At even that slight movement fresh blood welled in the gash. An ugly bruise had begun to form beneath the swollen lump.

The child watched her closely, waiting for an answer.

"Your name is Laban, is it not?" she asked.

He nodded.

"I do not know, Laban," she admitted. "I do know that Yahweh will not leave him alone. Not in this world, or the next."

Judging by his expression, her words brought little comfort. "What will happen if"—he swallowed and drew in a breath—"if he goes to the next world?"

Yahweh, help me comfort this child.

"Torah teaches that when our father Abraham died, he was gathered to his people. The same was true of his son, our father Isaac. Many say that we will leave this world and join our ancestors, our people, in the next."

Laban's shoulders slumped. "Imma and Adena and I are Abba's people too. We want him in this world."

Deborah resisted an urge to gather the child in her arms and comfort him. Instead, she formed a prayer. Though she intended to pray silently, her lips spoke the words in a whisper.

"Yahweh, this boy needs his abba. Dara needs her husband. Adena wants him to celebrate her wedding. Please have mercy on this family and spare him."

Doubt stabbed at her. Why had she spoken the prayer aloud? What would happen to the boy's faith if Chaim died?

In the next instant, the injured man's eyes moved beneath his eyelids. Hope flickered to life in her soul.

She leaned close to his ear. "Chaim? Can you hear me?"

A moan escaped the man's dry lips.

Sucking in an excited breath, Laban leaned close to his other ear and shouted. "Abba! Wake up, Abba."

A weight lifted from Deborah when Chaim's lips formed the words, "My son." Then he moaned even louder.

Merciful Yahweh, thank You.

Dara emerged from the house then with a clean linen cloth draped over her arm and carrying a bowl of water.

"Chaim?" She increased her pace to come to her husband's side.

Water sloshed out of the bowl. Deborah rose and relieved her of her burden, freeing her to rush forward.

"My wife." This time he breathed the words.

Dara threw her hands into the air and lifted her voice to the heavens. "Praise be to Yahweh."

Deborah set the bowl near his head and dipped the cloth into it. She squeezed water over the wound, and Chaim sucked in a hissing breath. His eyes fluttered open and then immediately slammed shut. A groan, the strongest yet, rumbled in his throat.

"Ach, the pain in my head. Was I kicked by a mule?"

"Abba," Laban shouted into his ear. "Not a mule. A man on a horse. He kicked you and you fell."

Chaim winced. "There is no need to shout." His eyes opened a slit, and this time they stayed open. "What man? And what is that smell?"

Deborah drew in a breath of smoky air. She had forgotten about the fire. A glance over her shoulder revealed at least a dozen people laboring in the northern part of the field, following the trail of the Canaanites. Behind them lay several rows of blackened wheat stalks, charred and smoldering, still sending streams of smoke into the sky.

"Never mind that now," Deborah told him with a glance at Dara, who nodded. Best not to upset him with details about which he could do nothing. "Rest and let your wife clean your wound."

She relinquished possession of the cloth and left Dara and Laban to tend to Chaim. As she approached the workers, Tivon and another young man beat the flames with mighty blows from blackened mats. A wave of smoke rose from the ground as the last of the flames were doused into nonexistence. The others gathered around the two, slapping them on their backs and murmuring congratulations in tired voices.

Sabra caught sight of her and closed the distance between them at a run. Soot blackened her cheeks and nose, and the hem of her skirt had been singed. She threw her arms around Deborah and buried her face in the soft part of her neck.

Deborah held her daughter close, feeling her body heave with silent tears. "Fear not, my little one. It is over. You have helped to save this family's field."

Lappidoth approached. Gray ash had settled on his dark hair, and his features were drawn and weary. For a moment Deborah glimpsed him as he would be when he was an old man.

"How is Chaim?" he asked.

The others gathered around, listening for her answer.

"Injured but awake." Deborah sought Adena's gaze. "With Yahweh's help, he will recover."

The young woman—girl, truly, since she had not yet bled—collapsed to the ground, weeping. Tivon knelt beside her, comforting her with strong arms and whispered words.

Gersham turned, looking to the north where the raiders had gone. "This cannot continue. How will we survive with our crops burned and our inheritance ruined?" He turned back to level a hard stare on Deborah. "Where was Yahweh when the Canaanites attacked Chaim? Has the God of our ancestors led us here to the land He promised our father Abraham, only to feed our enemies' lust for violence?"

Deborah felt the weight of every eye fixed on her. Inside the embrace of her arms, Sabra stiffened. *Yahweh, they look to me and expect an answer. But I am a woman. It is not my place to speak for You.*

Words rose up from her soul, but she clamped her teeth together. She was no prophet, no spokesperson for Yahweh. Why were they all staring at her, expecting a wise answer?

Lappidoth stepped near, his face concealed from all but her. A smile spread from his lips to his eyes, which warmed as they held hers. He dipped his head, as if to encourage her. Tension seeped from Deborah's taut shoulders.

"Yahweh will never leave us," she said. Gersham drew a breath to voice a protest, but she gave him no chance. "It is we who have left Him. Why do you expect Him to save you when you bow the knee to false gods?" Words burned in her chest, insisting to be spoken. "We have deserted our sanctuary and ignored His precepts. We have broken His mitzvah." She swept the onlookers with a sharp gaze. "How many of you have offered sacrifices to Baal? Have avoided the tabernacle, have broken *Shabbat*?"

Gersham lowered his eyes. Two of his sons sneered and turned away. Without another look at Deborah, Gersham joined them, and the three walked toward their home.

One son, though, remained. A handsome young man, the youngest of Gersham's sons. Deborah searched her memory for his name while he held her gaze in a haughty one of his own. A smirk hovered around the corners of his mouth. Uri. She remembered when he was born, though she had not seen him often since.

She directed her words at all the listeners but held Uri's eyes. "Yahweh led us to the land He promised our father Abraham. Though our ancestors disobeyed him and as a result were sold into slavery, He rescued them. He led them out of Egypt and set them free. Even then, Yahweh's people mistrusted Him. Broke His mitzvah. Allowed the gods of aliens to infect us." Unable to stop herself, she took a step forward, toward the young man with the haughty expression. "How, then, can we fault Him when we suffer the consequences of our lack of dedication to Him?"

Uri did not turn away from her gaze, as his brothers had. "It seems, then, that your God has abandoned us. Yes, we've strayed from the total devotion He demands." He splayed his hands wide. "Our fault, no doubt. Or rather, the fault of our ancestors." A grin twisted his lips, and Deborah had to admit, it was a handsome grin, though arrogant. He turned his head to spread his infectious smile around. "Are we to be accountable for the actions of people we do not even remember? What kind of God is this?"

Sabra, whose head had been resting on Deborah's shoulder, stiffened. She raised her head to look at him. With an arm still around her daughter's waist, Deborah felt her heartbeat quicken. A quiet alarm sounded in her head.

"You speak with authority," she told him, "though without wisdom of our people's history and our covenant with Yahweh."

"Perhaps you can instruct me. I have heard you know Torah well." His eyes lowered, and he fixed a gaze on Sabra that held a hint of something Deborah did not want to acknowledge.

Within her arms. Sabra straightened. Her young heart beat faster.

"I suggest you endeavor to study Torah, Uri son of Gersham," Deborah said. "Then you will learn what kind of God we serve."

Uri addressed Sabra. "Who teaches *you* about the kind of God we serve?"

A breath caught in Deborah's chest when Sabra uttered a breathless, "I—I—"

She pulled Sabra even closer. "She learns from her abba and her imma, as Yahweh instructed."

"Ah." He nodded, his gaze still fixed on Sabra. "I do not have the same…" He appeared to search for a word, and when he did, he filled it with heavy sarcasm. "…advantage."

Deborah fought to keep her answer civil. "The very reason I suggest finding a teacher."

"Perhaps I will." The smirk on those handsome lips deepened.

With an arm still around Sabra's waist, Deborah turned away and headed toward the house. When Sabra hesitated, she tightened her grip and pulled her away.

CHAPTER FOUR

Word of the most recent Canaanite attack spread, and the following day neighbors came to lend aid. While Dara tended to Chaim on a mat in the corner of their home, Deborah worked alongside the women setting the house to rights. In the family's storeroom, she knelt, picking up debris. The assailants had stormed through the main room, knocking jars and bowls off shelves and scattering the furnishings. The storeroom had been ransacked, and what little they'd left of foodstuffs littered the hard-packed dirt floor amid shards of pottery. Dara's broom had been used to beat the flaming wheat, which rendered it useless. Deborah sent Tivon to retrieve hers from home, along with a few rugs and mats to replace Dara's singed ones.

Dara's sister Elizabeth stood in the doorway of the storeroom looking over the mess and shaking her head. "They not only steal, they destroy what they do not take."

"I hate them," Malka said with a glare toward the northern wall in the direction the attackers had ridden.

Deborah looked up from her task. Malka's daughter-in-law Ophira had come to her for advice yesterday morning. "I am sure you do not mean that." She smiled to soften her rebuke. "Torah instructs us not to hate."

Elizabeth, who had long been a friend, picked up a shelf and set it on support brackets along one wall. "I think we finally found a place where you do not know Torah as well as you think." She grinned good-naturedly in Deborah's direction. "Were our fathers not instructed to destroy all the Canaanites who lived in the land Yahweh promised the children of the covenant?"

For a moment Deborah made no answer but picked up a broken jar. She held it at arm's length and watched the remnants of oil drip onto an oily mud puddle on the floor.

"Can this oil be salvaged?" she asked the room at large.

A snort sounded from Malka. "No. It is fouled by mud."

"Yes, it is," Deborah agreed. "The only oil that can be saved is that which has not been tainted by soil. Yahweh thought the same when He sent our ancestors into the Promised Land." She smiled up at Elizabeth. "The land He commanded us to conquer, to take from the pagan people who lived here. He knew if our people blended with the Canaanites, our purity and our devotion to Him would be contaminated. Rendered unusable." She tossed the broken jar into the rubbish pile.

Elizabeth chuckled. "You prove my point, my friend."

Deborah tilted her head as if in agreement. "But then, did He not instruct us, 'When you see the ass of your enemy lying under its burden and would refrain from raising it, you must nevertheless help raise it'?" She shook her head. "That is not the action of someone who is consumed by hatred. Instead, it is the action of one who is ruled by compassion. As is Yahweh, who is gracious, slow to anger, and abounding in kindness."

Elizabeth's chuckle burst forth in a deep-chested laugh. She pointed a finger toward Deborah. "I thought I had you, but you prove wiser. As always."

Malka's face betrayed her confusion, and Deborah prayed silently for words to settle her. But before she could speak, Tivon appeared in the doorway to the storeroom, his arms full.

"Here are the items you requested, Imma." He glanced around and then piled his burden on a wide table that Elizabeth had righted in the corner. "What else would you have me do?"

Deborah sat back on her heels. She noted he had brought her best broom, along with the woven rug that lay on the floor of his bedchamber and the spare mats she kept in readiness for guests who dined with them.

"I will have more to send later," she told him. "But for now, that is enough. See what you can do to help the others round up the scattered livestock."

He glanced over his shoulder. "Adena is fretting over the broken gate to the pen. May I help her secure it?"

"You may." He started to go, but a thought struck Deborah and she stopped him. "What of Sabra? Where is she?"

She had lost track of her daughter in the midst of the scurry of activity when helpers arrived and repairs began.

Tivon waved a hand in her direction, intended to relieve her worries. "She and Uri are carrying water from the well to the men who are digging up the burned wheat." He disappeared, off to help his betrothed.

Deborah's spine went stiff. Sabra was working alongside Uri?

She leaped to her feet. "I must go and…" In her mind she cast about for an excuse to leave. "And see to this family's evening meal. I will bring food from my own stores."

Ignoring the ladies' curious stares, she hurried from the storeroom. She would *not* leave Sabra in the presence of that idolator, Uri.

Deborah watched Sabra scrub a root vegetable with savage gestures. She had not been happy to be brought home to cook a meal.

"If you keep that up you will scrub the skin off." Deborah peered at her daughter's petulant expression. "You are angry with me."

Her young lips tightened. "You do not need me to make stew. I was helping the others."

"Helping Uri, you mean."

"We were in full sight of Abba." She slapped the vegetable on the work surface in front of Deborah. "You make it sound as if we snuck away together."

Deborah picked up the vegetable and applied a knife to chop it. "That young man is disrespectful. I prefer you do not spend time with him, even in front of the entire village."

"Disrespectful? Because he believes something should be done to put a stop to the attacks on our people?" Sabra turned to face her head-on. "Then I am also disrespectful, for I think the same."

Though outwardly Deborah continued calmly chopping, knots twisted in her stomach. While she understood the turbulent emotions of a girl approaching womanhood, she couldn't allow her daughter to treat her with open defiance.

She scooped up the chopped vegetable pieces and, after carrying them out to the dome-shaped tannur, added them to the stew. Steam wisped from the surface. She picked up the paddle and stirred, settling her thoughts before returning to the house.

"It may surprise you," she told Sabra, "to hear that I agree. These attacks must stop. If our people would forsake their idolatrous ways and return to Yahweh, He would act on our behalf."

Sabra made no answer. Deborah returned to her daughter's side at the worktable. "By disrespect I mean Uri's attitude toward our forefathers and even toward Yahweh. When he spoke of Yahweh, his voice held no reverence. By his words he demonstrated no understanding of our people's covenant." She placed a hand on Sabra's arm. "I would not have you dishonor your commitment to the God of our fathers by encouraging the attentions of one who has turned away."

The girl's cheeks reddened. "I did not encourage Uri's attentions."

Deborah folded her arms across her chest and held Sabra's gaze until the girl's head lowered.

"Perhaps he needs someone to teach him," Sabra said in a subdued voice. "He has only his father's example. His mother died when he was young."

She had a point, Deborah admitted. Lilah died giving birth to a daughter, who survived only a few days. After the death of his wife, Gersham turned his back on Yahweh. Deborah had been confined at home after giving birth to Sabra, but Lappidoth and others visited, took offerings of food and drink. When he returned, he told her Gersham cursed Yahweh for striking his wife with a fever. It was a wonder his sons knew anything of their ancestors at all.

"Perhaps he does." She lifted Sabra's head with a hand under her chin. "But that someone is not you. Uri son of Gersham is not the husband for you."

She knew she had hit upon Sabra's private thoughts when tears filled the girl's eyes. "It seems no one is."

Deborah's heart twisted, and she pulled Sabra into a close embrace. "There is one for you. Yahweh has selected the perfect husband. We will find him soon."

"Do you think so?" The words were muffled, spoken against Deborah's shoulder.

She poured confidence into her voice. "I know so."

Please, Yahweh, let us find him soon.

Oddly enough, an image of Uri, a smirk on his handsome lips, rose in her mind. She tightened her arms around Sabra.

I know You do not intend to give my daughter to an idol worshiper. You have someone else in mind for her, someone honorable and faithful to You.

In answer she sensed only a disquieting silence.

CHAPTER FIVE

Deborah carried a tray up the stairs to the roof, where Tivon and Lappidoth were seated. Sabra followed behind with a jug of milk, fresh from one of the she-goats. After the efforts of the past two days, a good meal of stew and bread with a cup of rich milk would help them all sleep soundly.

The sun hung low on the horizon, though it still shed enough light that they had no need for a lamp. Tivon rose at their approach and took the tray from her. She smiled her thanks as he set it on the rug. He'd been a handful as a child, but he'd become a thoughtful man. He would make Adena a good husband.

Her gaze slid to Sabra, who knelt on her mat to pour milk into their cups. They needed to find her a husband soon. Once the girl had a betrothed to focus on, she would forget all about Uri son of Gersham.

Again, a disconcerting prickle disturbed Deborah's spirit. What was this feeing? *Yahweh, what are You telling me?* But in place of the unmistakable assurance that often answered her questions, she sensed nothing.

When Sabra had placed milk in front of each of them, Deborah sat back on her heels and looked at Lappidoth. With the ash and sweat washed away, he once again looked like her beloved husband. No longer youthful, and never classically handsome, she admitted privately, but still the man she had loved for twenty years.

She'd first glimpsed him at her betrothal. Closed away inside her parents' house, she had peeked through a window while Lappidoth's abba and hers sat in the outer courtyard arranging the *mohar,* the bride price. The young man seated beside them was not what Deborah had hoped. His jaw was severely square, and his eyes wideset in a narrow face. Disappointment stabbed at her. She had prayed for a strong, broad-shouldered man, but instead saw a rather slight boy who plucked at loose threads on the sleeve of his robe, seemingly oblivious to the conversation that would affect them both for the rest of their lives.

In the next moment Lappidoth lifted his head and looked up. Deborah almost shrank back from the window until their gazes locked for one breathless moment. Then he grinned, and his face came alive. Dimples carved the cheeks above that square jaw, and humor twisted his lips. With one wink, he captured her heart. It had been his from that moment on.

Now, she watched him pick up a barley loaf and lift it toward the sky.

"Barukh ata Adonai Eloheinu melekh ha'olam borei minei mezonot."

As he prayed, Deborah recited the words silently. *Blessed are You, Yahweh, King of the universe, who creates varieties of nourishment.*

He tore the loaf in two and offered her half. Taking it, she brushed his fingertips with hers and then relished in the lopsided grin that never failed to entrance her.

"What a time we have had." He dipped his bread into the stew bowl and drew out a portion. "Good fortune was with Chaim. When I first saw him after the attack, I feared the worst."

"It was not fortune that saved him," Deborah said, dipping her own bread into the bowl. "It was Yahweh's mercy and power."

Tivon's face jerked toward her, eyes wide, a question clear on his face.

Deborah nodded but offered no explanation. None was needed. She knew all too well that she had played no part in Chaim's recovery. She merely sensed Yahweh's heart and expressed His will in her prayer.

"The raids are becoming more frequent." Lappidoth plucked a pair of olives from the tray and bit into one.

"At least here, in Ephraim, the Canaanites attack on horseback." Tivon tore off a piece of bread and dipped it in a dish of spiced oil. "We have a chance to defend ourselves. Whereas in the northern territories the raiders come in iron chariots. What defense can we offer against those?" He leaned forward, toward his abba. "Reuben told me he had news from distant family in Aphek that as many of our people die beneath the wheels of those chariots as by their swords." Creases wrinkled his brow. "And that the soldiers target children, who cannot run fast enough to escape."

"Tivon, please." Deborah spoke in a low but commanding voice.

When he looked her way, she slid her gaze toward Sabra, who had stopped eating and sat with her head bowed, her chin nearly touching her chest. The reports following the attack that killed Sabra's betrothed had been full of details of people dying beneath the wheels of those horrible iron chariots.

Tivon noticed his sister's sorrow and his expression became contrite.

Lappidoth leaned sideways to place a comforting hand on his daughter's shoulder. When she looked up, he gave her the wink that had captured Deborah's heart, and which she knew Sabra thought was hers alone. Deborah ignored a twinge of... something. Jealousy? No. At least not jealousy of her husband's affections. But perhaps a tiny bit of envy that her daughter took comfort from her abba when she so often lately rejected the same from her imma.

Tivon dipped his bread in the stew bowl. "Anyway, the attacks are much worse up in Naphtali and Zebulun. Reuben said the people cry out day and night for Yahweh to save them."

"Perhaps He will hear their cries, and ours," Lappidoth said.

Deborah shook her head, which drew a questioning look from her husband.

"Yahweh always hears the cries of His people," she said. "But cries alone will not move Him. They must cease their worship of pagan gods and honor the covenant of our father Abraham."

His lips curved in a smile. "You are right, as always."

They finished their meal in a tired but companionable silence. As she ate, Deborah watched the beloved faces seated around the mat and saw her own weariness reflected in theirs. They would all sleep well tonight.

The sun had faded to nothing more than a glow on the horizon while Deborah and Sabra covered and stored the remains of their meal. They joined Lappidoth and Tivon, who were seated on cushions and talking quietly about the events of the past two days. A flickering flame from the lamp between them set their faces aglow and created a circle of soft light. Their family's nighttime custom of gathering to recount stories and teachings from the past was one that Deborah cherished.

"I am sorry," Lappidoth said when she and Sabra sat. "I have no enthusiasm for storytelling tonight. My bed is calling to me."

Tivon agreed, yawning. "Morning will come too soon. Let us pray, Abba."

Ignoring a stab of disappointment, Deborah nodded. "Time to recite the evening prayer, then."

Lappidoth straightened and lifted his eyes to the ceiling in a posture of prayer. The rest of followed his lead.

"Blessed are You, Yahweh, King of the universe, who created day and night. You roll away the light from before the darkness, and the darkness from before the light. You make the bands of sleep fall upon our eyes and slumber upon our eyelids. May it be Your will, Yahweh, to let us lie down in peace and to let us rise up again in peace."

The familiar words resonated in Deborah's soul as she released the stresses of the day. As always, she became aware of Yahweh's presence in the words of the blessing, felt His pleasure in the faithful prayers of these four of His people.

The others rose and mumbled good night. She watched as Sabra and Tivon entered their bedchambers and let the curtains fall over the doorways. She rose to her knees then leaned forward and pinched the wick between her fingers. The circle of light disappeared. *You roll away the light from before the darkness.*

Lappidoth paused in the doorway of the room they shared. "Are you coming?"

Though moments earlier her eyelids had felt heavy, the presence of Yahweh during their prayer stirred deep in her soul. She longed to prolong her time with Him, to pray with her own words.

She rose and crossed the room to stand before her husband. "I think I would like to sit for a while beneath the tree." Peering into his face, she asked, "Do you mind?"

"No, beloved." His hand came up to cup her cheek in a gentle caress. "Take care."

He kissed her and then disappeared into their room. She listened to the sounds of him removing his outer clothing and climbing up onto the bedstead. Only when she ceased to hear movement did she leave the house.

Outside, the sun had truly disappeared. The moon glowed overhead and lit her path through the outer courtyard, where their five goats had settled on beds of straw in the corner. One raised its head and watched as Deborah crossed the courtyard and let herself through the gate. Their donkey, a sweet creature that was fatter than he should be due to the family's tendency to overfeed him, trotted over to nudge her with his velvety nose. She spared a moment to scratch his ears. Tivon's home, the one he was building for himself and Adena after their marriage, butted up against the walled courtyard to her left. It would be a small structure at first. Deborah smiled at the memory of his enthusiasm when he described how they could add more rooms when Yahweh blessed them with children.

The heat of the day had cooled, relieved by a breeze that stirred the grass at her feet. She gazed into the distance, where her destination was distinguishable only as a dark rise in the landscape against the night sky. Skirting the barley field, which took so much of Lappidoth's and Tivon's energy at this time of year, she passed through their small orchard of fig trees and paused near the long clay cylinders that housed her bees. Their melodious humming brought a smile to her face. Their symphony, subdued at night, never failed to soothe her. These bees worked hard for her and her family. And for Yahweh. The product of their labor not only provided honey but also the wax Deborah used to make wicks for the tabernacle in Shiloh.

She came to the foot of the hill and climbed the gentle slope. The ground here was stony and slanted, not useful for farming, but at the pinnacle stood a tall date-palm tree. Unlike an olive or fig tree, the palm had no branches or leaves. It grew sturdy and straight from the ground, and the fronds extended directly from the trunk. The fruit sprouted beneath the fronds and grew in clusters. When ripe, the dates were as sweet as the honey Deborah's bees produced.

She arrived at the top of the hill and laid her hand on the trunk. She liked to think of the palm tree as a symbol. The trunk stood for Yahweh, immovable and steadfast, providing nourishment for the fronds so they would flourish and bear fruit. The fronds represented the people of Israel, who only grew and prospered if they drew their nourishment from Yahweh, the Source of life.

Tilting her head back, she peered up at the abundance of foliage, smiling at the way the stars twinkled through the fingers of the fronds. Lappidoth had laughed and called her fanciful when she described the symbolism of the palm tree. But later that night he turned to her as they lay on the bedstead and told her he believed Yahweh had given her that image. She treasured the memory, because that had been the first time he acknowledged that she heard from Yahweh.

She lowered herself to the ground and rested her back against the trunk. Overhead the stars seemed to wink into being all at once, as if Yahweh had rolled away the darkness just as the words of their bedtime prayer said. A thousand pinpoints of light spread across the sky, each brilliant by itself. But together they cast a glorious light across the land.

Like the children of Israel. Each one is lovely, but they are only strong when they stand together, united as a covenant people.

A laugh burst through her lips. Yahweh liked to paint pictures for her, to help her understand His vision for His children.

When her laughter faded, a peaceful calm enveloped her like a blanket. She relished in the feeling for a long moment, listening to the faint rustle of the palm fronds and marveling at the beauty of the sky. The moon crept across the expanse, somehow brighter than before, as if not to be outdone by the stars. She lowered her gaze and scanned the landscape before her. From this vantage point she could see their land, and even the neighboring fields. In daylight she could glimpse Chaim's house and beyond, to the edges of their small village. Her house, the home that she had come to as Lappidoth's bride, lay below her, a dark cocoon for her sleeping family.

"Yahweh, watch over them as they slumber," she whispered. "Give them rest."

Her thoughts drifted through the events of the past two days. Ophira and her brother. Tima and her sons. The attack on Chaim and Dara's home. Gersham's disturbing statement, and his son's unwelcome focus on Sabra. And the disquieting silence from Yahweh when she prayed for a faithful husband for Sabra.

Now that she was alone, she could pour out her fears concerning Uri son of Gersham.

"Yahweh, we have raised Sabra to respect our people's covenant with You. We have taught her to revere You, and to keep Torah always." She struggled to put her thoughts into words. She believed that Sabra would stay true to the faith she and Lappidoth had instilled in her. And yet… "But she is young," Deborah admitted quietly. "I fear she will be lured away by that handsome young man who does not know You. I know that is not Your plan for her."

She paused, waiting for a reassuring nudge from within. Instead, she encountered only silence. A knot of worry lodged in her belly.

"Our father Moses taught us the mitzvah You gave so we may prosper in the land You have given us. Uri does not follow, or even understand the mitzvah."

More silence. She shifted her weight. An unsettling thought occurred to her. Was Yahweh's silence because He was unhappy with her question, or was it because of His intentions regarding Sabra and Uri?

Her mind skittered away from the idea. Uri was an idol worshiper. Like his own abba, he had turned his back on the God of their ancestors and embraced the false gods of the Canaanites. An image arose in her mind. She first saw a statue of Baal when she was just a girl, journeying through the countryside with her abba and imma on their way to visit family. In her young eyes the idol was terrifying. It towered high into the sky, taller than even her abba. In body it was shaped like a man but had the oversized head of a bull with cruelly twisted horns rising above its head.

She shuddered and wiped suddenly damp hands on her skirt. In her mind she heard her father's voice, quoting from Torah. *"An idol defiles like a creeping thing."*

"They sacrifice children to these statues." Her words came out as the faintest whisper, volume dampened by her horror. "Would You give my daughter to such a man?"

In the next instant, a soothing warmth washed over her, sweeping away the horror. She drew in a deep breath and with it, a sense of assurance. A word reverberated deep in her spirit.

Trust.

The knot in her stomach loosened, and she drooped against the tree. Yahweh asked only one thing of her—to trust Him. Words from Torah echoed throughout her. "*Yahweh will show you mercy and will have compassion on you. He will increase your numbers, as He promised on oath to your fathers.*"

In one rebellious corner of her mind, a thought niggled. *Why does Yahweh not say openly that He will place an obstacle between Sabra and Uri?* She pushed the thought aside before it could take root.

"I trust You, my King. Forgive my doubts."

As the words left her lips, her gaze was drawn upward. The stars seemed to pulse before her eyes. They blurred, and instead of a multitude of pinpricks they joined and became a mighty mass of light. She blinked to clear her vision, but the stars remained fused into a single, brilliant beam of radiance.

In the span of a heartbeat, her vision cleared. The heavens returned to their proper perspective.

Deborah realized her breath had caught in her chest and blew it out. Her heart pounded loudly in her ears, and she inhaled long, measured draughts of fresh air. Her mind whirled with questions. What had just happened? She knew with certainty that Yahweh had shown her something important. Was it about Sabra? About Uri?

No. She shook her head, as much to clear her thoughts as in answer to her own query. Not long ago she had looked upon the stars and imagined them as symbols of Israel, stronger united than separate. Then Yahweh had shown her what they would look like *truly* united. Powerful. Dominant. Mighty. A blinding force that could dispel any darkness.

Even the darkness of Canaanite idolators.

She drew her knees up and buried her face in her hands. Was Yahweh ready to act, to put a stop to the murderous raids His children endured? Did He intend to unite the Israelites against the Canaanite army?

Lifting her head, she whispered to the sky. "Why would You show this to me?"

The answer came as a random thought, a rogue idea that had no place in Deborah's world. But she knew the Source to be divine, because she would never think such a thing on her own.

Yahweh showed her, because somehow He intended to involve her in the coming conflict.

CHAPTER SIX

The vision of the united stars pressed on Deborah in the days that followed. She told no one, not even Lappidoth. How could she, when she did not understand it herself? Whenever her eyes closed, the image of brilliance in the night's sky blazed in her mind, and the certainty that Yahweh would soon move on behalf of His people took root in her soul. And that she had a part to play in His deliverance. She tried to form her thoughts into words, but anything she could say sounded arrogant and unseemly for a woman. So she stilled her tongue and maintained a near-constant silent prayer. *Yahweh, You are King of the universe. My life is Yours. Show me what to do.*

On marketplace day, the family rose early to break their fast so Deborah and Sabra could arrive at the village square in time to select a good spot. Deborah had assembled their wares in a neat pile by the door, and watched as the men loaded them onto the donkey's back. They left the house as the first signs of morning broke.

When they passed the home of Chaim and Dara, Laban burst through the door, shouting for their attention.

"Wait! Imma says can she and Adena walk with you?"

"They are welcome." They stopped, and Deborah asked, "How is your abba?"

Laban's eyes lit. "Abba says Yahweh healed him, and he keeps saying over and over, 'Praise be to Yahweh, King of the universe.'" He peered up at her. "You were there. Did Yahweh really heal my abba?"

She tilted her head as if in thought. "You were there as well. What do you think?"

"You prayed, and then he woke up." His eyes narrowed. "Did you do it?"

Though she did not look at Sabra, she became aware that the girl held her breath, waiting for an answer.

"Me?" Deborah threw her head back and laughed. "How could I heal anyone? I am merely a woman. It is from Yahweh that life flows."

At the sound of her laughter, Adena appeared from inside the house. "Did someone tell a joke?"

Deborah smiled at her son's betrothed. Such a lovely child, with rosy cheeks and delicate features. She would grow to be a beautiful woman one day.

"Not a joke," she said. "Your brother tells us your abba has recovered from his injuries and repeats his praise often."

"I do indeed." Chaim followed Adena out of the house with Dara at his side. "What else can I do but give thanks?"

The two made their way across the courtyard. Deborah could not help but notice Chaim's slow pace. An ugly purple bruise covered one side of his face, and he wore a fresh bandage wrapped around his head to cover the wound. But at least he still had breath in his body.

"May we travel with you?" Dara asked. "We have nothing to sell but much to buy after the attack."

"We will be glad of the company."

Adena and Dara each picked up a wooden yoke and balanced it across their shoulders. Empty bags hung from each end, ready to be filled with their purchases in the marketplace.

Dara instructed her son, "Help your abba. And do not forget to feed the goats."

They continued the journey with Sabra and Adena walking ahead, talking quietly together.

They arrived at their destination in good time and wound their way through the streets to the open area in the center of the village that served as a marketplace one day each week. Deborah glanced around the square. Already a half dozen or so people had laid out their wares, some on tables and some on woven mats on the ground. Her preferred place near the potter's shop had not yet been claimed, so she led the donkey there. Situated at a corner of the square, the location was easily visible to everyone. During slow times she enjoyed standing at the window of the shop, peeking inside to watch Yosef and his son at the wheel. She never tired of seeing them shape lumps of clay into items of beauty and industry.

Dara and Adena helped them spread out the knotted rug she always used and then arrange the goods they'd brought to sell. They lined small pots of honey along one side, next to a few jars of sweetened dates. Deborah's supply of the honeyed treat had dwindled, but she held hope the next harvest would provide enough to replenish their stores. Pride shone on

Sabra's face as she set out a dozen bowls containing cheese made from goats' milk and flavored with a blend of herbs and spices she had concocted herself. Deborah hoped people would buy the cheese for her daughter's sake, though privately she preferred a simpler, unspiced version. An assortment of waxed lamp wicks and beeswax candles, thick and sturdy for home use, completed their wares.

When they had finished, Deborah stood back and inspected their work. "We have not much to offer today."

Dara bent over to pick up a cloth-covered bowl. "Tivon told us how much he enjoys this cheese. What price are you asking?"

Deborah opened her mouth to offer the cheese as a gift but held her tongue when she saw pink spots erupt on Sabra's cheeks. She longed to be treated as a woman, and here was an opportunity. Let her enjoy the fruits of her labor. She nodded for Sabra to make her first sale.

After a pause, Sabra shook her head. "You are family." She smiled at Adena. "How could I take payment from my sister's imma?"

Deborah's chest swelled. A gracious reply, one to make a parent proud.

"Ah, but hard work deserves a reward." Dara pulled a small pouch from beneath her robe. "Two *gerah*?" She held a pair of coins toward Sabra.

Creases appeared in the smooth skin between Sabra's brows. She stared at the coins for a long moment. "One gerah only," she finally said and took a single coin.

Grinning, Dara returned the remaining coin to her pouch. "I appreciate your kindness, but you have much to learn about bargaining." She leaned forward and lowered her voice to impart a word of advice. "You are supposed to ask for more, not less."

Sabra responded with a grin of her own, and in that moment, Deborah saw in her the woman she would soon become. *Yahweh, take care of her. Guard her and guide her into the life You have planned, as You have done for me.*

The marketplace filled and bustled with people buying and selling. Daniel, the man from whom Lappidoth had bought two of their goats, arrived with a half-dozen doelings tied loosely together and proceeded to parade them around the square, offering them for sale or trade. Dara and Adena struck out in search of articles to replace their lost or damaged belongings. The sound of merchants calling out to shoppers rose above the chatter of women, many of whom came to the marketplace not to shop but to greet friends and catch up on news of their families.

By midday, half their wares were gone. To Deborah's surprise, news of Sabra's cheese had spread, and only two bowls remained. The girl glowed with pride.

"What will you do with your earnings?" Deborah asked.

Sabra tilted her head, thinking. "I think I will buy more herbs. I would like to try adding a little garlic, and perhaps tarragon."

Deborah kept a rein on her expression. Garlic in oil? Yes. But in cheese? Her stomach would revolt. But she merely nodded.

"And I need more bowls, and…" She glanced at a place behind Deborah. "I would like to visit Leah's table."

Deborah turned to look across the square, where Leah stood behind a table holding a display of brightly colored jewelry. She hid a smile. Sabra had always been fascinated with bracelets and headdresses. As a younger child, she had loved to parade around the house wearing the few pieces Deborah owned.

"Try not to spend all your earnings today," she advised, and was rewarded with an excited grin before Sabra rushed across the square. Apparently, jewelry took priority over herbs and pottery.

Deborah knelt before their rug and rearranged the remaining items in a more attractive presentation, filling in the empty places.

"Excuse me, Deborah?

She looked up at the quiet voice to find a young woman holding a baby. "Elana!" She rose and her arms stretched out automatically to take the infant. "I heard you had given birth. I trust all is well and the little one is healthy?"

Holding the warm bundle close, she peered into the tiny face. The baby slept, her delicate lips moving as if nursing in her dreams.

"She is well." Elana gazed at the infant with pride apparent in her tender smile. "I never knew how strong love could be until her birth. Sometimes Daniel and I lie on our sleeping mat with her between us just to watch her slumber."

Deborah nodded. "Lappidoth and I were the same with our firstborn. Daniel is pleased to have a daughter, then?"

"He hoped for a son, as all men do." She brushed a finger across the baby's whisper-soft hair. "But he loved Daniela from the moment he first held her his arms."

"Daniela?" Deborah smiled at the young mother. "He must be proud to name her so."

They stood admiring the baby.

"We leave in two days' time for Shiloh to bring my offering to the priests."

"You have completed your purification?" Thinking back to the day she'd heard of the infant's birth, Deborah counted the days. Threescore and six, as required by the mitzvah.

"I have." Elena lowered her gaze and went on in a shy voice. "I—I hoped to find you here today. Would you speak a blessing over Daniela?"

Surprise slackened Deborah's jaw. "The priests at the tabernacle will bless this little one if you ask them to."

"I know," she said. "And we will, but can a child have too many blessings?" While Deborah searched for a reply, she hurried on. "You have studied Torah, and you are wise in the ways of Yahweh. Ophira told me she came to you for advice, and you helped her. I thought if Yahweh trusts you to give wise counsel, He will surely heed your blessing on my child."

Thoughts whirled in Deborah's mind. Parents recited nightly blessings over their children, and often other relatives blessed them as well. Other adults in the same Israeli tribe often offered words of blessing for children. Nothing in Torah prohibited blessings. But to seek one from an outsider?

Yahweh, may I give this child a blessing?

In answer she felt a rightness in her spirit. Yahweh cherished each child born in Israel.

"I agree with you," she replied. "Can any of us have too many blessings?"

A relieved smile curved Elena's lips.

Deborah pulled the infant close in one arm and placed a hand on the baby's head, covering the soft black curls. Lifting her eyes to the sky, she recalled from memory the words of the blessing the priests in Shiloh spoke over her children.

"May the One who blessed our ancestors Abraham, Isaac, and Jacob, Sarah, Rebecca, Rachel, and Leah, bless this child, whose name in the house of Israel shall be Daniela, daughter of Daniel and Elena. May Yahweh guard her from all evil, grant her a long life, and establish the work of her hands. May her father and mother rejoice in her and help her learn to become a blessing to her family and to the family of Israel." She removed her hand and then, on impulse, placed it upon Elena's head. Words from Torah rose from inside. "'And Yahweh spoke unto Moses, saying, speak unto Aaron and his sons, saying: on this wise ye shall bless the children of Israel. Ye shall say unto them: Yahweh bless thee and keep thee. Yahweh make His face to shine upon thee and be gracious unto thee. Yahweh lift up His countenance upon thee and give thee peace.'"

Where had that second blessing come from? Elena had not asked for it, and Deborah had not intended to speak it. But when she withdrew her hand, she found tears glistening in the young mother's eyes.

"Thank you," Elena whispered.

Deborah transferred the swaddled infant to her mother's arms. "May your travels be safe."

She stood still watching Elena leave. *Yahweh, You never fail to surprise me.*

A male voice sounded from behind her. "So."

Turning, she looked into the disapproving eyes of Asif son of Jonah.

"Are you now selling blessings along with candles?"

"Certainly not," she answered, appalled at the notion. "Yahweh's blessings are freely given."

He fired another question at her, the words dark with censure. "You claim now to be a priest?"

Her stomach tightened beneath his glare. With an effort, she replied in a steady voice. "Is it only priests who may bless Yahweh's little ones?"

"Those were the words given to Aaron and his sons, Israel's first priests," he snapped. "That is a priestly blessing."

"And yet many times my father spoke the same words over his children. Have you never uttered those words over your own family?"

He ignored the question. "You are a *woman*." The disdain he gave the word made it sound like a curse.

An acerbic reply rose to her lips. *How observant of you.* She bit the remark back and worked hard to maintain a calm demeanor. "Does Torah forbid women to bestow blessings? Tell me where, that I may learn."

His only answer was a furious snort blasted from his flared nostrils. He turned his back and stomped away.

Deborah stared after him, willing taut nerves to settle. *Yahweh, what have I done to earn that man's hatred?*

"I seem to have happened upon an argument."

Turning, she found Uri nearby, watching Asif's retreating form. His snide expression sent a different kind of tension through her. How had a young man become so arrogant and condescending? Sabra's words returned to her. "*His mother died when he was young.*"

"Not an argument," she replied, turning away from his smirk. "Merely a discussion about Torah's instructions regarding blessings."

"And the role of priests, and of women."

Though she refused to look at his face, still she heard disrespect in his tone. She made no answer, but instead knelt before the rug to rearrange the unsold pots of honey.

"I have thought about what you said."

She switched the placement of two candles. "And what was that?"

"That I should study Torah."

Her hand halted, hovering over a pot. Was he serious, or was this merely an attempt to lure her into another contentious discussion? "What thoughts have you had?"

Instead of answering, he said, "My brother Elias says you are a fool, and I am doubly a fool if I listen to you."

Ah. A jab, as she suspected. She would not rise to his argument. "Does he?"

"And my brother Zeb says you and those like you hold fast to a restrictive creed that has no bearing on our people today. That the God you revere is no different than Baal or Ashcrah or any of the others."

He spoke the words as if quoting them verbatim, though still in the arrogant tone that set her teeth on edge.

When she could speak calmly, she asked, "And what does Gersham say?"

A long silence followed. Curious, Deborah turned her head to look up at him. His face betrayed no emotion at all.

Finally, he answered. "Abba says I am of an age that I may make my own choices." He shrugged and went on indifferently. "And if I wish to follow a God who strikes down women and children, I may do so under my own roof but not his."

A response fashioned from years of bitterness and anger. The man must have been truly devastated at the loss of his wife and infant daughter. He blamed Yahweh for his tragedy, had hardened his heart, and had raised his sons to do the same.

Sabra ran up to them. Coming to a stop, she greeted him with a breathless, "*Shalom.*"

The snide smirk once again twisted his lips. "When I saw your imma here alone, I feared you had stayed home."

"I was just…" A flush rose in her cheeks. She held up a cluster of garlic.

Alarms sounded in Deborah's ears. The girl was too flustered to speak, obviously enamored with his attractive looks and not yet mature enough to discern his disagreeable nature.

"And is this a new purchase?"

He extended a hand, and his fingers brushed a pendant suspended from a cord around her neck. The intimate gesture brought Deborah to her feet in an instant. By the time she stepped to Sabra's side, Uri had dropped his hand and retreated to a proper distance.

Sabra grasped the pendant, her eyes shining. "It is."

Deborah drew herself up to her full height, which put her almost on level with the young man. "What brings you to the marketplace today? Are you here to trade, or merely to—" She snapped her mouth shut on the rest of the sentence. *Or merely to plague me and try to entice my daughter with your charms.* "—gossip with the women?"

She was instantly ashamed of her veiled insult.

If Uri noticed, he chose to ignore the taunt. He answered Deborah's question without taking his gaze from Sabra. "I have a taste for honey, and I have heard yours is the sweetest in all of Ephraim."

Sabra's face flamed, while the unspoken meaning set a different kind of fire blazing in Deborah. A dozen harsh words not befitting a devout woman battled to escape her lips, and she stopped them only by clamping her teeth together. *Yahweh, set a guard on my tongue.*

Acting as if she were completely oblivious to the undertones, Sabra answered, "It truly is the best." She hurried to the rug and picked up one of the two remaining bowls of flavored goat cheese. "If you like cheese, you might try this. It is blended with herbs." She lowered her eyes, her lashes fluttering the tiniest bit. "I made it myself."

The twisted smile deepened. "Then I am certain it will be delicious." He took the bowl. "What is your price?"

Sabra glanced at Deborah, her eyes dancing. "Three gerah." Then she bent to pick up a small pot. "And three for the honey as well."

Deborah gaped at her, surprised. All morning they had set the price on two gerah each.

With no hesitation, Uri said, "A bargain." He pulled six coins from a pouch hanging at his side and held them out to Sabra.

Creases appeared in her brow, and she cast an uncertain glance at Deborah. "You are supposed to offer half that amount, and then we will settle on a price between the two," she told him.

"Is that the way it works?" The question held a hint of humor, and a touch of mockery as well. "No matter. I have agreed to the price, and I have no wish to haggle with one as lovely as you."

Obviously pleased, Sabra's chest heaved with shallow breath. When she made no move to take the coins, Uri approached Deborah. Her hand rose almost without thought to take the payment. Then he took the honey pot from Sabra's unresisting fingers, dipped his head in a farewell to both, and struck off toward the far end of the square.

Deborah finally found her voice. "Uri," she called after him.

He turned, his brows arched with a question.

"How did you answer your abba?"

The infuriating sneer returned with force. "I told him I am fond of having a roof over my head."

He sauntered off, while Deborah's hands clenched into fists. Nothing could ever compel her to give her sweet daughter to one such as Uri son of Gersham.

CHAPTER SEVEN

Deborah swept the goats' soiled straw into a pile in the corner of the courtyard. Tivon had turned the livestock out to graze when he and Lappidoth left after the morning meal. Sabra found the task of cleaning the goats' pen distasteful and had begged to work in the house instead, on her newest batch of flavored cheese.

Piling the smelly straw onto a measure of cloth, Deborah permitted herself a chuckle. She could hardly blame the girl. Her success in the market two days past had encouraged her to try even more daring combinations of herbs and spices.

The sharp odor wafting from the straw stung her nostrils as she bent to gather the ends of the cloth and tie it into a bundle. Lappidoth would work it into the earth after the current crop of barley was harvested, where it would blend with the soil and somehow encourage a more plentiful harvest next season. How that happened was a mystery to Deborah, but she marveled that in Yahweh's world nothing was wasted. Even the most repugnant items could be turned to good use.

"Shalom," a nearby voice called to her.

She straightened and saw a couple approaching from the direction of the village. They came to a halt on the other side of the stone wall that encircled the courtyard. The woman carried a child on one hip, a boy of perhaps two years with an abundance of black curls covering his head. The man, who looked to be no more than a few years older than Tivon, carried a pack slung across one shoulder. She had never seen them before.

"Shalom," she replied.

The man's gaze dropped to the pile of waste at her feet before he spoke. "We are looking for Deborah, the wife of Lappidoth. We were told we could find her here."

Her curiosity piqued, she said, "I am Deborah."

The man laid a hand on his chest, fingers splayed. "I am Levi, and this is Anna, my wife."

Anna kept her eyes downcast while she dipped her head in a silent greeting. The little boy stared solemnly at Deborah.

She smiled at him. "And who is this?"

"This is Tobias," he replied. "He is…our son."

"A handsome child," she commented. The child had his abba's eyes and the shape of his mouth.

Anna looked up. Gazing into the young woman's eyes, Deborah felt her heart snag. Pain lay plainly in the brown depths. But then she again lowered her head.

Her husband adjusted the pack on his shoulder. "We come from Hadid, to the east of here. We arrived yesterday." He paused and pursed his lips several times in what Deborah realized was a nervous gesture. "Hadid is north of Gezer and south of Neballat."

Definitely nervous. *Yahweh, why did You send them here? How can I serve them?*

She maintained a pleasant expression. "I have heard of Hadid."

His feet shuffled on the dirt path. "We learned in the village that Deborah—that you are a wise woman. We came in hopes that you will advise us."

This couple, these strangers, came seeking her advice? Though friends and neighbors did so often, she had never been sought out by people she did not know. She became aware that her robe was soiled from her work, and she probably smelled as bad as the straw she had just bundled.

Wiping sweat from her brow with the back of her hand, she gave a small laugh. "As you can see, I am hardly in a shape to welcome guests, though—"

"We can come another time." Anna spoke for the first time, her expression now anxious. "We do not want to interrupt your work."

Deborah glanced at the smelly pile and grinned. "I will consider it a great favor if you would interrupt this work. It is not the most pleasant of tasks." The pair visibly relaxed, and Deborah gestured toward the house. "Please be welcome."

The doorway stood open in hopes of coaxing a breeze inside. Deborah led them, aware as she entered that the house reeked of garlic. She bit back a chuckle. What must her guests think to come seeking advice only to have their noses assaulted with such strong odors as garlic and goat dung?

Sabra stood at the other end of the common room before the worktable, chopping garlic. She looked up when they entered.

"This is my daughter," Deborah told her guests. "Sabra, this is Levi and Anna and Tobias, who recently traveled from Hadid. Would you see to their comfort while I clean up?"

Sabra's face brightened to be trusted as woman of the house, even for a short while. "Yes, Imma."

Deborah picked up a bowl and dipped water from a jug on her way to the sleeping room. Once there, she quickly stripped off her soiled tunic and scrubbed the worst of the sweat and grime from her body. She spared a grateful thought that she and Sabra had recently washed the family's clothing as she selected her favorite dress.

When she returned to the common room, she found Anna and Levi seated on mats near the open doorway, sipping from cups, with a plate of bread and a bowl of cheese—garlic flavored, no doubt—on a tray before them. Sabra sat cross-legged beside them with Tobias in her lap. She had retrieved a toy from her bedchamber, a spinning disc with two holes, through which a strip of leather had been threaded. Deborah remembered the day Lappidoth brought the toy home and gave it to Sabra, who had been little older than Tobias. On each side of the disc the craftsman had carved a deer. The child watched, fascinated, as Sabra wound the disc tight, and then pulled both sides of the leather strip. The disc spun, making it appear as if the deer was running. Delighted, Tobias laughed, and his mother beamed. Watching her brought back memories of Deborah's own joy at the musical sound of her babies' laughter.

She retrieved a woven mat and settled across from the couple. "Tobias is a happy boy."

"He is." Anna's tone held something more than merely acknowledgment. Gratitude? Relief?

They watched while Sabra played with the child, who was entranced with the toy. Sabra seemed to enjoy the play as much as Tobias. One day she would make a fine mother. Emotions battled in Deborah. Pleasure at the thought of her daughter with children of her own, and uneasiness at the question of those children's parentage. Who would their father be?

When the couple made no move to speak, Deborah did. "What errand brings you here, so far from your home?"

The two exchanged a glance, and then Levi spoke. "We came in hopes of finding a home. We have none of our own."

Deborah watched the young man as he spoke, saw distress plainly in his eyes. This, then, was the reason they came seeking advice. Something had happened to drive them from their home in Hadid.

"We are a small village, but a peaceful one." Faces paraded in her mind's eye, reminding her that not everyone in the village lived peacefully with one another. Asif. Gersham. Uri.

"We have our conflicts, as all people do." Then she became serious when she remembered recent events. "We suffer from Canaanite raids, as I believe most of Israel does, though not nearly so often as those who live closer to the northern borders of the land Yahweh gave our fathers. But in general, this is a good place to raise a family."

Again, the two exchanged a glance, this one longer. As she watched, Anna's eyes slid to Tobias and then locked onto

Deborah's. The meaning was clear. They did not wish to talk in front of their son. Or maybe Sabra.

She drew a breath. "Sabra, perhaps Tobias would like to see the olive trees." Turning her attention back to Anna, she added, "They are in full bloom, and lovely."

Rather than irritation at the suggestion that she leave the adults to talk alone, a wide smile broke out on Sabra's face. "I think he would. Come, Tobias. I have something to show you."

She stood up, settled the boy on her hip like any mother would, and left the house, talking to him all the while in a low voice.

"Thank you," Anna said quietly. "The advice we seek is not for young ears."

As Deborah had suspected. She nodded for them to continue.

Levi appeared to struggle for words. When he did speak, he did not meet her eyes.

"My abba died three years past. We are a family of wood-workers, and he trained all his sons in the trade."

"How many brothers do you have?" Deborah asked.

His jaw became rigid, as if enraged by that simple question. "Four," he finally ground out. "I am the second son. My father was the youngest of six sons."

That explained much. Torah stated that the firstborn son should receive a double share of the father's inheritance. The youngest son of a large family would receive only a small portion of his father's inheritance. Levi's father, or perhaps grandfather, must have taken up a trade to support his own family, since the land he inherited might have been too small to farm. And Levi, being the second son, would likewise inherit only a portion.

He had fallen silent, his brows pulled low across his eyes as if struggling with an unpleasant memory.

"Did you and your brothers work together?" Deborah asked.

"We did. Until…" His throat moved as he swallowed. Looking up, he blurted, "Tobias might not be my son."

Anna gasped, and the pain that erupted on her face nearly broke Deborah's heart.

Yahweh, give me wisdom. Show me how to help them.

Levi snatched up her hand, immediately contrite. "I mean, he *is* my son. He is ours."

For the next few moments Deborah felt like an outsider while the two engaged in a silent conversation. At a very slight nod from Levi, Anna spoke.

"Levi's abba was a kind man. When we married, he welcomed me into his family and treated me as if I were a beloved daughter."

"You *were* a beloved daughter to him," her husband insisted. He had not released her hand. "He loved you more than any of my brothers' wives."

"And I loved him." Tears filled her eyes. "My sisters-in-law were jealous of the kindness Abba showed me. And they shared that jealousy with their husbands."

"And with Imma," Levi added, and Anna again nodded.

Deborah clearly saw the conflict. When the father died, his patronage of Anna was removed. The women of the family would have no reason to veil their jealousy and dislike. She might even have been poorly treated.

"You shared a home with your family?" Deborah asked.

They both nodded, and then Levi took up the story. "Asher became head of the family and of our woodworking shop. Though he married a year before me, his wife is barren."

Deborah's gaze strayed to the doorway, through which Sabra had carried Tobias. "When you became with child, her jealousy flared."

Anna's face crumpled, and she shook her head. "No. I mean, yes, but…"

Levi squeezed her hand and continued in a wooden tone. "One day the women went to the marketplace and left Anna at home to take care of the household. Asher left our shop, claiming he had an errand. He went to the house."

Horror crept over Deborah. Her hands rose to cover her mouth while her mind supplied the details the couple did not share. Was Tobias the son born of Asher's detestable violence on his brother's wife?

Tears streamed down Anna's face, and her shoulders shook with silent sobs. Levi put an arm around her and pulled her close to his side.

"She did not tell me." Now tears also wet Levi's face. "She was afraid I would do harm to my brother. And she was right. I would have killed him with my own hands. Instead, she lived in fear, forced to face him day in and day out. Even after Tobias came, she held the secret close."

Yahweh, this is more than I can manage. Only You can bring peace and healing to those who have suffered such brutality.

How she managed to speak in a calming tone, Deborah did not know. "When did you discover your brother's betrayal?"

"A few weeks back," he said. "Asher became drunk and claimed that Tobias was not my son, but his. His firstborn. He demanded that we give the boy to him and his wife. A terrible fight ensued." His eyelids slammed shut, his features tortured. "Asher fell into a drunken stupor. We gathered our belongings and left under the cover of darkness."

During the silence that followed, Anna sobbed softly while Deborah lifted a wordless petition to Yahweh. Words from Torah rose up from memory, not words of comfort but mitzvah that this couple might find difficult, even cruel.

Give me Your wisdom, Yahweh, for I have none of my own.

After a long moment, during which her spirit reached out to the heavens, she opened her mouth, uncertain of the words she would speak. "When you approached my house, what word did you use to greet me?

"I said, 'Shalom.'"

"You spoke a blessing to me, that I might be filled with peace. And I answered with the same, wishing peace upon you as well."

A bitter breath blasted from Levi. "I am told you are a wise woman, but how can peace be possible when my wife has been treated so unjustly? When I have been treated unjustly by my own flesh?"

Deborah's heart cried out in agreement. *Yahweh, how can Your peace rest on these two?*

Again, she spoke, not certain of the words but confident that they came from a divine Source. "Shalom does not mean merely the absence of conflict. Yahweh's shalom is complete. It is wholeness. It means to restore that which has been stolen from you."

"How?" Anna nearly shouted the word. "No one can restore what was taken from me. Not you and not anyone else. No one can remove the memory of pain and disgrace, of—" A shuddering sob choked off her words.

Deborah leaned forward, across the tray, and grasped her hand. "You are right. I cannot restore your shalom." Anna looked into her eyes, and Deborah held her gaze. "But there is One who has power to accomplish what no man or woman can. Torah was given to bring shalom to all. It is full of teachings about shalom and how to grasp it. By obeying the mitzvah Yahweh gave to our fathers in the wilderness, we can embrace the true shalom that comes to us only by His hand."

Peering into Anna's eyes, Deborah saw the moment when a tiny particle of hope crept in among the agony.

Her gaze slid to Levi. "You both can know shalom that sinks deep into your soul and spreads throughout your members."

The edges of his lips turned downward, and he shook his head slowly. "Abba was loving and generous, but he did not follow the teachings of Yahweh. Nor did his abba before him. I know little of Torah."

"My abba taught me." That flicker of hope in Anna's eyes grew, a light amidst the darkness of her desperation. "I do not remember much of the mitzvah."

Deborah released her hand and sank back again on her heels. "Following Yahweh's mitzvah is not always easy."

Levi's eyes narrowed. "In what way?"

She tilted her head. "Consider this teaching. Yahweh commands: 'You shall not hate your brother in your heart; you shall not avenge or bear any grudge.'"

He threw up his hands in disgust. "That is not possible. How can I not hate him for what he has done?"

"For you it is impossible," she agreed. "But not for the King of the universe. I believe Yahweh's purpose in giving us Torah was to show us how to grasp shalom and live in harmony with one another." He watched her closely, and she could almost see the thoughts flitting through his mind. "Do you not see how this hatred, this grudge, is hurting you? Your family? When you lie down at night, do you feel turmoil and unrest?"

His gaze dropped. He answered in almost a whisper. "Yes. I do see."

"That pain, that anguish is not what Yahweh wants for you." She glanced at Anna. "For either of you. Your suffering does not affect the one who inflicted this pain on you. It affects you." She leaned forward again, the words tumbling across her tongue while the truth she spoke swelled in her spirit. "It is only by devoting yourself to the Lord your God and His teachings that you can be set free from your misery. Leave your brother to Yahweh. Do what is right for you and your family."

"My abba recounted the stories of our ancestors," Anna said. "I remember some of them. Of Abraham and Sarah. And of Jacob and his son Joseph and…" She drew in a quick breath, her eyes suddenly wide. "And how his brothers mistreated him and robbed him of his freedom." She turned toward Levi. "His *brothers*."

Deborah could hardly contain a victory shout. "Do you remember what happened to Joseph after his brothers sold him as a slave?"

A smile, a real one, broke out on her face. "Yahweh gave him wisdom. And riches. And then there was a drought, and his brothers were starving and came to him for help."

"Did he help them?" Levi asked, caught up in the story.

Anna's eyes sparkled. "He did. And he forgave them." She went on, awestruck by the ancient story. "They abused him and he forgave them."

Deborah could not hold back a grin. "Only Yahweh could restore him and reconcile him to his brothers."

Levi shook his head. "I do not seek reconciliation, nor would I welcome it. But I long for this shalom of which you speak." He reached for Anna's hand. "For my family."

"Will you teach us?" Anna straightened, excited by a thought. "If we settle here, will you teach us Torah?"

The question took Deborah by surprise. Her, teach Torah to strangers?

And why not? I taught to my children everything I learned from my abba. I have had opportunities to study what most woman do not have. And Yahweh has blessed me with a memory so that I can recall all the words I have been taught.

The idea nestled like a seed in her spirit and began to sprout before she had drawn two breaths. She could teach Torah. And she wanted to.

To Anna and Levi she said, "I will consider your request. I must speak with my husband and pray for Yahweh's guidance before I answer."

A sound from outside reached them, the sound of a child's cry.

Anna leaped to her feet. "Tobias!"

Before Deborah could react, she had dashed through the doorway. Deborah eyed Levi, aware that she had been left alone in her house with yet another man. She started to stand but then hesitated. Could she say something to begin this young man's healing?

"Does your brother look like you?" she asked.

Levi looked surprised for a moment before answering. "No. He has the look of our abba, while everyone always remarks upon my resemblance to Imma."

Deborah would not go so far as to ask whether marital relations continued before and after the terrible attack. That would not only be unseemly but unforgivably intrusive. Instead, she made a comment in what she hoped was a casual tone.

"Tobias resembles you to a remarkable degree. I would venture to say when he is grown, he will look like your twin."

She watched his expression as he considered her words and saw the moment when the hard line between his eyes softened. The corners of his lips twitched upward.

"Thank you," he said.

Before she could answer, Anna returned carrying Tobias, with Sabra following close behind.

"He caught sight of the donkey and ran toward it," Sabra told them. "He fell."

"He is unharmed," Anna added. "A scrape on his knee is all."

"The first of many, no doubt." Levi extended his hands toward the child, who nearly launched himself out of his mother's arms. "You must learn to keep your balance before you run, my son."

When Levi lifted him high in the air, Tobias squealed with laughter. A sudden rush of joyful tears blurred Deborah's vision. This family had taken a step toward the shalom that was their birthright as children of Israel. She could almost feel Yahweh's smile.

CHAPTER EIGHT

That evening Sabra chattered to Lappidoth about their visitors while Deborah put together the family's evening meal. From outside came the sound of Tivon tapping a mud brick into place on his house.

"Tobias loved the olive trees. He said 'pretty flower.' And we played with the deer disc, and he laughed so hard his little face flushed red."

She spoke with such enthusiasm Deborah paused in the act of slicing an onion to watch her.

"Did you let him take it with him?" Lappidoth asked.

Sabra's face fell. "No. I did not think of that." Then she brightened. "I will the next time I see him. He will be here often since Imma is to teach his parents Torah."

Lappidoth turned a searching look on Deborah, and she chopped with renewed energy. She had not yet told him about the couple's request.

"Deborah?" her husband asked. She looked up. "What is this?"

"I planned to discuss the matter with you later," she said.

She pursed her lips and caught Sabra's eye. The girl lowered her head.

"They came from Hadid, and plan to settle here. Levi is a trained woodworker, and they hope to open a shop in the village. Someone there told them to come to me for advice over a…" Her gaze slid to Sabra and then back to Lappidoth. "Over a sensitive matter."

He understood and nodded. "And Torah?"

She resumed her work, thankful to have a task to keep her hands busy. Though she would much prefer to have this conversation privately, the question had been asked, and she owed her husband an answer.

"The young man was raised in a family in which Torah was not taught. When I explained the mitzvah that would govern their sensitive matter, they asked if I would teach them." She lifted her shoulders. "That is all."

Sabra must have sensed Deborah's desire to speak alone with her husband, for she quietly rose and left the house, presumably to help her brother.

"And what answer did you give?"

"None. I told them I would consider the request." She looked up so he could see her honesty. "And that I would speak with my husband and pray for guidance before I gave an answer."

He considered that. "And have you prayed?"

"I have." In truth, she had done little else since her visitors left. As she worked, her mind maintained a constant prayer that Yahweh would reveal His answer.

"And?"

She set the knife down and came around the worktable to where he sat cross-legged on a mat. She dropped to her knees before him. "These Torah lessons are Yahweh's plan for me,

Lappidoth. I am certain of it. The knowledge consumes me like..." She closed her eyes and searched for words to describe the rightness she felt, the absolute conviction that Levi's and Anna's request had come directly from heaven, and that once the lessons began, her feet would be set upon a path laid out by Yahweh Himself. Opening her eyes, she held his gaze. "Like the sight of the burning bush must have consumed Moses." When he would have spoken, she rushed on. "Before you say yea or nay, I must tell you one thing."

She outlined her conversation with the couple and ended with the fact that she had once again found herself alone in the house with a man.

"It was for moments only," she told him. "It happened so quickly that I had no chance to prepare or to object."

His silence stretched so long that Deborah clenched her hands into fists to keep her fingers from twitching with impatience. Finally, his lips softened into a tender smile.

Encouraged, she asked, "Will you share your thoughts with me?"

"I was thinking of that day twenty years past, when I sat in a stranger's courtyard and saw for the first time the girl who was to be my wife. If I had known she would one day become a teacher of the Law—"

"Not just the Law," she hurried to say. "I will teach them Torah, all the stories from Adam to Noah to Abraham and beyond. For it is through our ancestors' examples that we learn of Yahweh's faithfulness and our own failures."

Laughing, he held up two hands, palms facing her. "You need not teach me. Save your lessons for those who have not been raised to know them."

Muscles that she did not know were clenched wilted, and she sank back on her heels. "You agree?"

"Am I to disagree with the King of the universe?" He made the statement lightly but then sobered. "But you must take care, Deborah. You must not open yourself to gossips and accusation from such as Asif."

"I beseeched Yahweh about that very thing, and He provided a solution." The idea had come so suddenly and complete that she knew the Source to be divine. "I will sit beneath my palm tree for a period each day. On the hill, in sight of you and Tivon and anyone who cares to see. I shall let it be known that I welcome any who would learn."

Lappidoth's soft smile broke free, and the skin around his eyes crinkled. "The perfect answer to any naysayer. When will you begin?"

Such joy welled up in Deborah that she launched herself forward and threw her arms around his neck. Laughing, he tumbled backward and, holding her tightly, rolled sideways.

When he kissed her, she formed an unspoken prayer of gratitude for the gift of such a husband.

Then she pulled back and asked, "What about that time twenty years past? Had you known what this day would bring, would you have refused to marry me?"

His hand came up to caress her hair. "I would have fallen on my knees before Yahweh and thanked Him for the treasure He was about to bestow on me."

He pulled her head toward him and kissed her again, this time so tenderly that she nearly wept with love for him. Then she buried her face in his neck and relaxed in his arms.

Deborah knelt on the ground and plucked an errant weed from the small plot of vegetables she tended in the enclosed space behind their house. The morning clung to the cool of night, and the occasional breeze that washed over her held none of the searing heat of the week past. She lifted her head and breathed deeply, inhaling the scents of spring. The barley harvest would soon be upon them. Lappidoth would gather the first sheaf and would travel with it to Shiloh, where he would present it to the priests during the Festival of Unleavened Bread, as Yahweh commanded. It was a journey Deborah always looked forward to, a place to gather with representatives from all tribes of Israel.

This year she would remain at home. She and Lappidoth had discussed it as they lay on their bedstead the night before, after he had given his consent to her plan to teach Torah to Levi and Anna. She would celebrate Passover here, with them, and that would be a valuable lesson during which she would recount the mighty act of Yahweh in delivering the Hebrew people from tyranny and slavery in Egypt. Though she would certainly miss the journey to Shiloh, already details of her lesson and her meal flitted through her mind.

"Deborah? Where are you?"

Lappidoth. She thought he was working in the fig orchard with both of their children. She lifted her head to answer his call. "Tending the vegetables."

"Come, please. We have a guest."

A guest? She got to her feet, wiping her hands on her apron, and hurried around the house through the courtyard, where she found Lappidoth and their guest, Yadon son of Nahir. He farmed his family's land, which lay on the north side of the village. She offered a smile and a nod of greeting. What business did he have with Lappidoth?

"Would you prepare refreshment for our guest and join us on the roof?" Lappidoth asked.

"Certainly." She aimed a smile at Yadon. "Are bread and honey to your liking?"

He returned the smile. "Your honey is famous. I would be honored to taste it."

The men ascended the stairs, and she entered the house to do as requested. While scrubbing the dirt from her hands, she wondered about Yadon's visit. A trade, perhaps? He farmed lentils, which, like barley, were harvested in early spring. Such a trade would augment their food stores and give their meals variety. She would welcome such a trade.

When she had assembled a tray, she carried it up the stairs and found the men seated in the shade of the canopy.

Lappidoth nodded his thanks when she set the tray down and poured wine into cups. She picked up the first and extended it toward their guest.

"Yadon wishes to discuss a betrothal between him and Sabra," Lappidoth told her.

The cup wavered in her fingers. She turned a wide-eyed stare from her husband to Yadon, who rescued the cup before she could drop it.

"I understand the offer is unexpected," he said.

She reviewed the particulars she knew about him. Some years past he married a cousin from a village near the northeast border of Ephraim. She had been younger than he by ten years or more and bore their first son within a year of the marriage. The second son arrived the following year. The poor girl died giving birth to a third child, a daughter. How long ago was that? Several years at least. Yadon's imma, who still lived in the family home though her husband had gone to rest with his ancestors even before Yadon's marriage, had arranged for a nursemaid, the widowed daughter of a distant cousin. The woman, Eden, brought her own suckling infant with her and cared for them both. Deborah had seen Eden often in the marketplace and thought her an admirable woman.

Lappidoth leaned forward to pick up his glass. "Yadon's daughter is nearly two. Her nursemaid says the child will be weaned before the fall harvest."

Deborah held her tongue. What had the child's feeding habits have to do with Sabra?

"When that happens, Eden will return to her family in the north." Yadon appeared to struggle for a moment before continuing, clearly reluctant. "I offered marriage to Eden. My children love her as the only mother they remember. She refused me."

So Sabra was not this man's first choice as wife. But why did Eden wish to leave Yadon's house? And might that reason affect Sabra as well? Would she be unhappy if she made her home there?

She worded her question carefully. "Is Eden unhappy here in our village?"

He sipped from his cup. To delay answering while he formulated an acceptable reply?

"A message arrived recently from her abba in the north." His glance included them both in the explanation. "The son of a distant cousin is of an age to marry and has inquired after her. Her abba wishes her to return with her child at the soonest possible moment."

Lappidoth lifted the dipper from the honey jar and drizzled golden liquid over a piece of bread. "My daughter is only twelve and not yet a woman. It may be some time before she is ready to become a wife. Only Yahweh knows the season of such things."

As though he had anticipated the comment, Yadon answered without hesitation. "I hope, once we are betrothed, she might consent to caring for my children a few days each week, that they might come to know her and she them. And she can be of help to my imma as well." He directed an explanation to Deborah. "Her hands swell and cause her such pain she cannot lift food to her mouth."

"Eden feeds her as well as the children?" Deborah asked.

"Yes. She is as kind and gentle as if Imma were her own." He lowered his gaze, his expression troubled. "We shall miss her when she leaves."

His plight was now clear. Eden had become far more than a nursemaid for his infant daughter. She was tasked with the care of the entire family, young and old alike. More than likely she also ran the household, since there was no one else capable of taking on that responsibility. He needed to find a replacement for when she left. And he had chosen Sabra.

"I have amassed a substantial mohar," he hurried to tell Lappidoth, who merely nodded and bit into his sweetened bread.

Yahweh, is this Your answer to our prayers? Is Yadon the husband you have selected for my Sabra?

Faced with silence, Yadon lifted his cup and drained it. When she noted his unsteady hand, compassion stabbed at Deborah. Circumstances had left him with small children, an ailing imma to care for, and no abba to negotiate a betrothal.

Lappidoth finished his bread. "We will think on the matter."

"And seek Yahweh's guidance," Deborah added.

Yadon gave a quick, jerky nod. "Yes, of course."

With a smile, Lappidoth told him, "Sabra is our only daughter, you see. We are anxious to see her well settled."

"I understand," the younger man replied quickly. "I—I would give her a good home. A good life. My farm prospers, and I am not a harsh man."

Lappidoth held up a hand to stop the flow of self-commendation. "I am certain you would. Now, you have not tasted my wife's bread and honey. Please." He gestured toward the tray. "Enjoy our refreshments, and tell me of your farm. You will harvest a good crop this year?"

Talk of the betrothal had come to an end. Deborah excused herself and returned to the garden. After twenty years of marriage, she knew Lappidoth well. He would not agree to anything regarding their daughter without consulting her.

The visit ended sooner than she expected. When she heard her husband bidding Yadon farewell, she left the garden and hurried to the front of the house in time to bid him farewell.

Standing side by side, they watched him leave. Only when she was certain he was out of earshot did she turn to Lappidoth.

"What are you thinking?"

He cocked his head to one side. "It is a good match. While he is not wealthy, he is prosperous. Sabra would be well cared for."

"He has two sons," Deborah pointed out. "No son of Sabra's would be his heir."

His lips twisted as he considered that. "But she would be close. We would still see her and her children. We could have meals together and celebrate the festivals with her."

At his wistful tone, Deborah looped her hand around his arm. He would miss his daughter when she wed and left their house. Far better, in his eyes, to have her close than to marry her to someone who would move her far away.

"I think he has feelings for Eden," she said.

His eyebrows rose. "The nursemaid?"

"She carries a much heavier burden in that home than nursemaid. His regard for her is apparent."

"But she is set to marry another," he reasoned.

Deborah could not deny it. Besides, love was not a consideration in marriages. Love grew as the couple matured. She had no doubt that whoever Sabra married would grow to love her and that she would grow to love her husband in time, as Deborah herself had.

"Shall we put the matter to Sabra?" she asked.

He drew in a breath. Though it was customary to obtain the bride's consent regarding her marriage, the choice was not hers to make. Children lacked the maturity to make wise decisions. It fell to the father to ensure that his children were cared for.

Finally, he nodded. "We will discuss the matter with her tonight."

───────────────

"No!"

Deborah winced. Sabra screeched so loudly the sound might have carried from the roof of their home to neighboring farms. The noise of Tivon's work on his house ceased, proving he had heard the outburst.

Deborah, Lappidoth, and Sabra were seated beneath the canopy on the roof, the same place where they had entertained Yadon son of Nahir.

"Sabra." Deborah used the stern voice that had told her children, when much younger, they had best stop whatever mischief they were into. "You will not use that disrespectful tone."

Chastened, the girl lowered her head. "I am sorry, Abba," she mumbled. But then her head shot up. She clasped her hands and held them beneath her chin. "But I beg you, do not make me marry him."

"Sabra," Lappidoth said in a much gentler tone than Deborah's, "it is a fine offer. Yadon has proven himself to be hardworking and dependable. His farm is profitable. As his wife you would lack for nothing. And he honors the faith of our forefathers."

Tears welled up in her eyes and spilled over. "He is *old*."

"Not yet thirty," Lappidoth answered. "He is strong and healthy. He will be able to give you many children."

The tears fell faster. "He will die years before me and leave me a widow." She drew in a shuddering breath. "Why can I not marry someone who will take care of me when I am old?"

Lappidoth's expression softened, as it always did for his only daughter. Deborah knew she must insert herself into the conversation, to be the strong one.

"Age is of no consequence," she said, though she relaxed her tone. "As your abba said, Yadon is healthy and hardworking. You will be much better off than many girls your age."

Sabra did not take her gaze off of Lappidoth. "You are only a few years older than Imma." A sob shook her thin frame.

"The marriage will not happen soon," he told her. "Not until you are a woman. You have a year, maybe more, to become acquainted with him. And the children. Consider how you enjoyed the child who visited yesterday."

"That was di—di—different." Her breath shuddered with the force of her sobs. "He belonged to someone else." She fell to her knees and prostrated herself before him. "Please, Abba, do not make me marry him. I will do anything, anything."

Lappidoth lifted his gaze to Deborah over the girl's head. The look he gave her was filled with helplessness. Tenderness for him flooded her. She knew then that he would not force his daughter into a marriage about which she had such violent feelings. And the knowledge brought relief.

Deborah knelt and placed a hand on her Sabra's back. "Sabra." She spoke in a softer tone than before, and the girl lifted her tear-stained face. "Go below. Wash your face and compose yourself. Leave us to discuss the matter."

Sabra cast a desperate look at her abba but then nodded and left the roof. Once again the sound of Tivon's work ceased, and Deborah imagined her telling her brother the news.

Deborah sat beside her husband, close enough that their thighs touched, so that they might draw comfort from one another.

"I do not have the heart to force her," Lappidoth confessed. "And she is correct. Yadon is closer to my age than hers. She may very well spend years as a widow, and then who will take care of her?"

"Her children." She grasped his hand. "As Yahweh intends."

He agreed with a nod, but still his features betrayed his struggle. "I had hoped for a different match. One where she and her husband may grow and learn together. I have no doubt she would come to love Yadon's children, and perhaps him as well. In time." He shook his head sadly. "In his house, she will have no time."

He spoke the truth. Sabra would be thrust into a household where she bore the brunt of the work not only for his children but the care of his imma as well. She might very well grow to resent them all but would be powerless to do anything. Was her future to be full of bitterness and helplessness?

"I want only our daughter's happiness," she told him.

He searched her face, and tension visibly faded from his. "Then we are in agreement? We will reject Yadon's offer?"

Yahweh, guide us.

She searched her thoughts, her feelings. Then she nodded.

"We are in agreement." But then a thought burst upon her and with it a heavy load of concern. "I fear she holds out hopes for Gersham's youngest son."

"No. Our daughter will marry into a family that is true to our beliefs. To Yahweh."

Relief flooded her. "A second matter on which we are in agreement." She squeezed his hand. "But we must find a suitable husband for her soon."

Resigned, he nodded. "I will send word to my family in Gezer and the hill country of Aphek."

"And I to my sister in Shiloh," Deborah said. "Perhaps between all our relatives we can find the husband Yahweh has selected for her."

"Yes," he agreed, though glumly. "But I wish there was someone nearby. I will miss her when she is gone."

Yet another thing on which they agreed.

CHAPTER NINE

On *Richon*, the day after Shabbat, Deborah left her house to conduct her first Torah teaching. She had selected the noon hour, which gave her time to finish her morning tasks.

When she stepped outside, her gaze flew to the hilltop. A flutter erupted in her stomach upon seeing five figures walking toward the palm tree. Five? From this distance she could not make out their features.

Lappidoth appeared from behind Tivon's house. "Your students are ready."

Surprised to see him home at this time of day, she said, "I thought you were tending the barley."

"I left Tivon and Sabra working. I would like to go with you today." He opened the courtyard gate and stood waiting for her to join him. "Unless my presence will unnerve you."

"I will be glad of your company." She glanced toward the hill again and confessed, "Truthfully, I feel a bit...hesitant."

Laughing, he put an arm around her waist. "There is no need for nerves. You know Torah better than many scholars. Simply tell them what you know."

Bolstered by his nearness, she felt the quivering in her stomach calm. Together they climbed the hill. When they neared the top, Levi caught sight of her.

"Shalom, Deborah," he said as he came toward her.

"Shalom, Levi. This is my husband, Lappidoth." She laid a hand on Lappidoth's arm. "And this is Levi, the woodworker I told you about."

"Shalom." Lappidoth's welcoming smile put her further at ease.

"Shalom," the younger man answered. To Deborah he said, "I hope you do not mind if we brought our new friends to hear your teaching."

She looked at the four adults standing behind him and recognized them all. Seth, a leather worker who lived on a corner of his father's land west of the village, whom she had known since she came here newly married to Lappidoth. His wife, Rachel, stood beside Anna. With them was Rachel's imma, an elderly woman she had met only a few times in the market. She had come to live with Levi and Rachel not long ago when her husband died. The last of Deborah's nerves fled.

"I am honored," she told them. To Levi she said, "I am happy you have made friends here."

"We met by chance," Levi told her. "When Seth heard that we were in need of a place to stay until we can find a home of our own, he kindly offered a room in their house. In return I will build new wooden racks for his leather craft."

Deborah smiled at Seth and Rachel. "How kind of you. You model the hospitality of our father Abraham, who opened his house to strangers so they might have food, drink, and a place to rest their heads."

Rachel's mother turned to her daughter. "And there you have it. She knows the stories of our ancestors, stories many have forgotten in this wicked day." She faced Deborah. "My father taught us about Abraham and Isaac and the rest. But my husband was a harsh man and could not abide such talk." She put an arm around Rachel. "I want my daughter and my grandchildren to learn."

Deborah cast about for the woman's name. When it came to her, she smiled. "Perhaps you can tell a few of the stories yourself, Shira."

But Shira waved the suggestion off. "I have forgotten more than I ever knew. I have hopes that your teaching will stir my memories."

Lappidoth spread his arms wide to indicate them all. "Let us sit and be comfortable."

Deborah went to the palm tree and sat where she often did when praying, with her back to the sturdy trunk. The others found places before her.

Yahweh, give me Your wisdom, Your words.

"Before we begin our study of Torah, we must ask Yahweh's blessing on the teaching." She lifted her hands to the heavens. "Blessed are You, Yahweh, King of the universe, who hallows us with mitzvah, commanding us to engage with the words of Torah. Sweeten the words of Torah in our mouths and in the mouths of Your people. Blessed are You, Yahweh, who teaches Torah to His people."

She lowered her arms and settled them in her lap. Her gaze slid from face to face. What she saw there emboldened her. Six eager expressions, all fixed on her, awaiting the word of Yahweh.

Confidence filled her. Lappidoth had spoken truly. She knew Torah, and she revered Yahweh. Nothing else was needed.

She lifted her chin. "We will begin at the beginning of all things. The beginning of Torah is called *Bereshith*." Drawing a breath, she pulled the words from memory. "In the beginning, Yahweh created the heaven and the earth...."

As harvesttime approached, Deborah's following grew. The number of those who came to her daily teachings expanded to include dozens from the village and surrounding lands. Lappidoth no longer accompanied her up the hill to the palm tree, for the fields required his attention, but the nerves of that first teaching had not plagued her again. How could they, when she immersed herself in the words of Torah?

On a day some weeks after that first lesson, she climbed the hill with her thoughts focused inward. Today she would recount the lineage of Noah's sons. Not the most exciting of lessons, but she must show how Yahweh's people increased and how they spread across the land. And how those peoples became the ones they knew today. How Noah's son Ham fathered Canaan, from whom came the Amorites, the Jebusites, and others that made up the peoples known as Canaanites, for it was only then that they would—

She came to a halt as she crested the hill. Before her, seated in the open area stretching from her tree onward, were more people than she could quickly count.

Upon seeing her, Levi stood and hurried toward her. "It seems word of your teaching has spread. Visitors from the south, from Hebron in Judah, have come to hear."

Before she could respond a stranger approached. "Shalom, Teacher."

"Shalom," she replied.

"I am Amram, from the tribe of Judah. With me are men from Hebron on our way to Shiloh to worship at the tabernacle there." He waved toward a group of unfamiliar men seated behind those she knew. "We have heard of a teacher whose wisdom rivals that of the prophet Ehud and thought to stop on our journey to listen."

She kept a tight grip on her jaw so that it would not dangle open in astonishment.

"I am honored," she said and formed a mental prayer of thanksgiving that bewilderment did not sound in her voice. To be compared to the famed judge of Israel sent her thoughts reeling. The vision of the stars rose again before her mind's eye. Could Yahweh have such lofty plans for her as He had for Ehud?

"I hope we do not intrude."

"All of Yahweh's children are welcome here," she said.

Amram bowed from the waist and returned to his clansmen. Deborah turned to Levi, whose eyebrows twitched upward. Then he shrugged and rejoined his wife.

Deborah scanned the faces of those from her village. She caught the gaze of Dara, who sat beside her son Laban. The boy had not missed a teaching in weeks. Dara gave her an encouraging smile and a nod.

Then her gaze snagged on a new face, one she recognized. Seated a short distance apart from the others was Uri. He wore the arrogant smirk that irked her so. When he knew she had seen him, the smirk deepened. What had brought him here today?

She approached the palm tree and sat beneath it. The sturdy trunk, which she imagined represented the strength of Yahweh, bolstered her. A hushed silence fell over the assembly, all of them watching her. She shut her eyes and formed the prayer that she prayed every time she sat beneath this tree.

Yahweh, give me Your words, Your wisdom.

A sensation of peace, of quiet confidence, soothed the last of her anxious thoughts. Opening her eyes, she lifted her hands to the heavens and began.

"Blessed are You, Yahweh, King of the universe...."

* * *

Deborah drew the session to a halt at the ninth hour with the closing blessing.

She lifted her hands and spread her arms wide to encompass the entire group. "*Hazak, hazak, v'nithazek.*" *Be strong, be strong, and let us strengthen each other.*

Those who had attended before recognized the dismissal. They began gathering their belongings, and soon the others followed their example. Deborah stood and stretched, pressing a hand against an ache at the small of her back. This had been the longest lesson yet, because so many had questions. Unlike the priests in Shiloh, who did not tolerate interruptions, she gave each one her attention and tested the answers in her spirit until she became certain her words held Yahweh's wisdom.

Ophira hurried toward her with an eager expression. "My brother arrived three days past."

"Yosef consented to teach him the ways of a potter, then?" Deborah asked.

The young woman nodded. "He and my Reuben have welcomed him. Tyrek began his apprenticeship yesterday."

"Did he enjoy the work?" Deborah asked.

Ophira's smile dimmed. "Not especially. He told me his hands were awkward and his efforts clumsy compared to Reuben's. I reminded him that Reuben has had his hands in clay since he was old enough to sit on his father's lap at the wheel, and that he must continue to learn and practice." She lowered her voice so as not to be overheard. "He swore to me on oath that his errant ways are behind him. I pray that is the truth."

Several men approached from the crowd and waited behind her, among them Amram of Hebron.

Deborah placed a comforting hand on Ophira's arm. "Let us pray your brother feels more confident each day."

When Ophira stepped away, the men took her place.

"You are a wise teacher," Amram said. Then he cocked his head to one side and peered at her from beneath heavy, dark eyebrows. "Where did a woman learn Torah?"

She studied him warily. Was the question intended to challenge her knowledge? In his expression she saw nothing but genuine interest. The men with him waited for her answer.

"I was raised in Shiloh, the eldest of five girls," she told him. "My abba worshiped Yahweh with unwavering devotion and loved Torah. He taught me to do the same."

"He was a priest, then?" the man beside Amram asked.

She shook her head. "He was a stone cutter in his youth, but an accident left him without the use of one hand." Unbidden, her right hand clenched into a fist at the mention of Abba's crooked fingers. "He spent long hours at the tabernacle, listening to the priests read from the holy scrolls. I always accompanied him and hid behind the linen curtains to listen. Then as we walked home, we discussed what the priests had read."

A look of admiration colored Amram's features. "I see the hand of Yahweh in your learning. Your teaching is sound and your answers wise."

Deborah lowered her head. "All praise be to Yahweh."

"We must be on our way on the morrow, but we will stop here again."

She looked up to find his companions nodding.

"I look forward to your return," she said.

"Until then, shalom."

She lifted her hands and spoke a blessing. "May the God of our ancestors Abraham, Isaac, and Jacob lead you in peace to your destination. May Yahweh protect you on your leaving and on your return and rescue you from harm. Shalom."

Amram accepted the blessing with a nod and then stepped away. His companions followed, save one. Deborah looked into the man's face and saw reverence shining in his eyes.

"Your wisdom stands alongside that of Othniel, Ehud, and Shamgar."

Her breath caught in her throat. This man compared her to the great judges of Israel, who led Yahweh's people in wisdom and in warfare. The vision of the stars erupted again in her mind.

"Could Yahweh appoint a woman to lead us?" His eyes held hers. "Until today I would have said no."

He turned and followed Amram, leaving Deborah numb.

But only for a moment. Another man took his place, and this face held no reverence.

She blinked away the vision. "Uri son of Gersham."

"Shalom." His condescending tone belied the meaning of the word.

"When I saw you, I could not help but wonder. Have you changed your mind about living under your abba's roof?"

"No." He gave no further explanation but narrowed his eyes to study her. "You spoke of the descendants of Shem, Ham, and—" He scratched his head.

She supplied the name. "Japheth."

With a nod of acknowledgment, he continued. "You said the Canaanites came from the line of Ham. But Ham's abba was Noah, who was also the abba of Shem. And Abraham was of the lineage of Shem."

"I see you listened to my teaching," she said.

He tilted his head to acknowledge her comment. "Would that not make the Canaanites our brothers? And if that is true, why did Yahweh tell our ancestors to drive them out of their land?" The irritating smirk deepened. "Why are Shem's descendants more worthy than Ham's?"

The tone with which he spoke, more than the question itself, set her teeth on edge. He did not come today to learn. He came to find fault with her teaching and mock her with it.

And yet was that a spark of interest she detected behind the sneer?

She chose her words with care. "Your question is a good one."

A flash of surprise wiped the arrogance from his face, but only for a moment.

"The answer lies a bit later in our people's history. Since I am teaching Torah in the order in which it is recorded, you will discover the answer in the next two or three lessons."

His eyes rolled upward. "So I must continue coming?"

Giving him a sweet smile, she said, "Only if you want answers to your questions."

His shoulders heaved with a silent laugh, but he said nothing more. Merely turned his back on her to leave.

"Uri," she called after him.

He stopped and looked back at her over his shoulder.

"Why *did* you come today?"

His lips twisted. "I thought Sabra would be here."

She drew in a sharp breath and opened her mouth to deliver a scalding rebuke, but he sauntered away, laughing.

CHAPTER TEN

The spring harvest was upon them. Deborah suspended her daily sessions to help with the barley. As always, their nearest neighbors also came to help.

"A fine crop you have this year," Dara said as they worked.

Deborah straightened from her task and looked out over the field. Golden stalks, their tops heavy with grain, stretched before her. They danced in a light breeze, the movements a wave that wafted across the field.

"Yahweh is merciful," she told her neighbor. "Lappidoth fretted that the hot spell a few weeks past would do damage." She broke off the head of a nearby plant and broke it open between her teeth. The hull broke with a satisfying crack, and the seed inside held its shape under the force of her fingernail, indicating the plant was perfectly ripe for harvest.

Ahead of them, Lappidoth and Chaim worked with sickles, cutting the stems close to the ground. The women followed at a safe distance, gathering the stalks into bundles and tying them with thin strips of leather. Behind them lay a row of sheaves drying in the sun.

Deborah glanced to her right, where Tivon also yielded a scythe, followed by Adena, Sabra, and Laban. Though the boy had wanted to cut with the men, Dara deemed him too young to handle such a sharp instrument. Reluctantly, he had joined the girls. Beyond them, at the edge of the field, stood a tithe's portion of unharvested barley left, as Torah instructed, for the poor, that they may feed themselves.

After gathering an armful of stalks, Deborah pulled a strip of leather from a pouch at her side. She knelt to secure the sheaf. A large one, perhaps even the one Lappidoth would take to Shiloh for the Feast of Unleavened Bread, to present it to the priests as an offering to Yahweh. They would not eat any of the new harvest until this offering had been accomplished, in accordance with the mitzvah given to Israel.

"Deborah, look."

Dara stood with a hand shielding her eyes, looking into the distance. Deborah straightened and then smiled when she saw a group of people traveling in their direction.

"It is Levi and Seth," she said through her smile. "And Yosef and Reuben and—" She strained her eyes and noted that their wives walked with them. Most of these were regular visitors to the palm tree teachings, though the young man walking beside Ophira was not familiar to her. "That must be Tyrek, who was recently apprenticed to Reuben."

"And the men carry sickles." Dara grinned at Deborah. "With their help, we will make short work of this harvest."

Lappidoth had seen the newcomers. He and Chaim ceased their labor and waded through the golden barley to meet them. Deborah left her work as well to join them.

"Shalom." Lappidoth's greeting rang with welcome. "Do I dare hope you have come to help with our harvest?"

"We have, my friend." Yosef, the eldest of the group, strode forward and grasped Lappidoth's arms with both hands. "We are tradesmen and therefore have no field to harvest." His glance fell on Deborah, and he added in a hearty voice. "And we wish to show our gratitude to the wise woman who opens Torah for us."

She planted her hands on her hips. "I have not seen you in the gathering before my palm tree," she teased.

"What need have I, when my son's wife recounts your teaching each night over the evening meal?"

Deborah turned a smile toward Ophira, who watched the exchange with dimpled cheeks. She rejoiced to hear Yosef's words. If her students left the tree and told others what they had heard, then Yahweh's truths would spread throughout Ephraim. Perhaps even through all of Israel, if Amram and others like him returned.

"We are grateful for the help." Lappidoth spread his arms wide to include them all. "Thank you, and welcome."

They spread out through the field. Yosef sang as he worked, his deep voice ringing across the land. The familiar words of his song, sung by her family during festivals in Shiloh, stirred Deborah's memories. She joined in, and though her voice was not nearly as fine as his, her heart rejoiced at singing praises to the King of the universe. Within a few words, other voices merged with theirs. Levi paused in his work to listen, delight apparent on his face. Since his abba did not follow the teachings of their ancestors, she doubted if he had ever heard such songs.

Some time later, Deborah stopped her work to survey their progress. With so many hands sharing the task, the harvest would be complete in just a few days. She formed a prayer of thanksgiving for each person present.

Beside her, Dara finished tying a sheaf and stood. "I would welcome a drink of cool water."

Deborah agreed. "And when the day is done, they will be hungry. I will prepare a meal for them. A small enough reward for their labor."

"A fine idea," Dara said. "May I help you?" She put a hand to her back and winced. "I would much rather stand over a cookstove than bend over another barley sheaf."

Deborah looped an arm through hers, and together they walked toward their husbands to share their plans. As they did, she caught sight of a lone figure approaching. Her good humor wilted when she recognized him.

"Asif." She spoke quietly, in a tone filled with dismay.

Dara squeezed her arm. "Perhaps he has come to help." She winced at a look from Deborah. "Though probably not."

Lappidoth had seen him as well. He turned and caught Deborah's eye and then headed toward their visitor.

Dara patted her arm in sympathy. "I will go to your house and begin preparations for the meal."

Nodding, Deborah headed across the field, weaving her way around bundled sheaves of barley. She met Lappidoth at the edge and drew comfort his placid expression. Together they waited for Asif's approach.

He spoke while still a few steps away. "I see you have hired workers for the harvest."

Lappidoth answered in a pleasant tone. "Not workers. Neighbors who offer their labor out of friendship." He paused and glanced at Deborah. "And out of gratitude."

The man's thick eyebrows crashed together. "Gratitude for what?"

"For my wife's teaching." Lappidoth smiled at her. "She has assembled quite a following of men and women who desire to learn more about Yahweh and His mitzvah."

"Yes, men." His features darkened with a glower. "That is the reason for my visit." He turned his glare on Deborah. "It is indecent for a woman to teach men, and yet you do it openly."

"Indecent?" She glanced at her husband, who nodded for her to continue. "You accused me of unseemly behavior when I offered advice to a young man who came to my house seeking wisdom. And now you accuse me of indecency when I offer Yahweh's wisdom in the open, surrounded by His creation."

"Yahweh's wisdom?" His voice rose. The sound of the sickles hacking at barley stalks behind her ceased. "You are a woman. What do you know of Yahweh's wisdom?"

Lappidoth answered, "She knows and cherishes every word written by the hand of Moses. Why should she not share her knowledge with those who do not?"

Asif whirled on him, his fury growing. "You should exercise control over your wife. Is it not written that Yahweh's hands formed the man, but the woman he drew from the man's side?" He focused on a point behind them. "And does Torah not say that the father will teach his son the words of Torah? Not the mother but the father."

Aware that their friends had stopped their work to listen, Deborah answered in a clear tone, "And what if the son does not learn from his abba? Is not the learning more important than the teacher?"

His gaze swept her from her head to feet. "You are a woman. You must not teach men."

"From where in Torah does this prohibition come?" she asked. "Or does it merely come from the law of Asif?"

A male chuckle sounded from behind her.

The flush in Asif's face darkened to purple. "It is being spread about that you proclaim yourself to be a prophetess, and Israel's next judge."

"That is not my claim." She lifted her head and held his eye. "Though some of those who sit under my teaching have suggested the title may be Yahweh's intention."

"And how do you respond?" he snapped.

She maintained a calm demeanor in the face of his scowl. "That we will know Yahweh's will when He reveals it."

"Why did you not deny them that instant?" He lifted his head and shouted to those in the field. "This is heresy! Is it any wonder Yahweh has turned His back on us and allowed the Canaanites to abuse our people? Yahweh would never bestow the wisdom of a prophet on a woman."

"And yet he has." The voice belonged to Seth. "Before you claim to know what Yahweh has and has not bestowed, you should come to Deborah's palm and hear her teaching."

"I?" Asif slapped his hand to his chest, outraged. "Never. I would not risk Yahweh's displeasure by participating in such blasphemy." He stabbed a finger at Deborah. "You must stop spreading your woman's advice among the men of this village and return to your house and become obedient to your husband. Else you will suffer the wrath of our righteous God." His nostrils flared with distaste. "And I pray it will be soon."

He whirled and stomped in the direction from which he had come.

Deborah did not move. The confidence that fueled her answer to his hostile accusations fled, replaced by tears prickling her eyes. She would not turn and let her friends see how the man's words had unnerved her.

Lappidoth addressed those standing behind them in a light voice. "I had hoped he came intending to join us in our work, but it appears not." A subdued laugh answered him. "Let us dismiss those distasteful words and turn our thoughts to Yahweh. Yosef, have you another song?"

"Certainly."

The words of yet another song of praise rang out in his melodious voice. Soon others joined in, and the sound of work returned.

Lappidoth put an arm around her shoulders. "You do not answer to Asif, Wife. Remember that."

She blinked back her tears and looked up into his face. "Do I dishonor you by answering the call of Yahweh?"

His arm tightened and drew her close. "Put that thought from your mind. I feel nothing but pride in the wife Yahweh has given me."

The words rang with truth, and yet Deborah sensed something else, something behind the words.

"And yet?" she prompted.

"I do miss the peaceful life we enjoyed before," he admitted. "I hold out hope that peace will return to us one day. Before your attention revolved around the next day's lesson." He left her to return to the work of the harvest.

Deborah headed toward the house to get on with the task of preparing a meal for their friends, but his words troubled her. Deep inside, she knew Yahweh had plans to disrupt their peaceful lives far more than He had so far.

Deborah and Dara served a plentiful meal to their tired but cheerful friends. The evening being mild, they formed a circle with mats and rugs in the grass beyond the courtyard. Deborah opened her stores and did not scrimp on the stew, adding a generous portion of dried mutton as a special treat. Besides the stew, she served bread, olives, dates, and several varieties of Sabra's cheese.

"It is a feast," Lappidoth exclaimed when the workers arrived from the field.

Levi rubbed his hands together, eyeing the food trays with obvious delight. "It is indeed. Had I known my teacher had such talents in the kitchen, I would have offered myself as a laborer before now."

Laughing, Anna gave his arm a playful slap. "This one is always hungry," she told the others.

"We have Dara to thank for the stew," Deborah told them. "She has a way with spices."

"My wife will be sorry she did not join us," Yosef said.

"You will take a portion home to her when you leave," Deborah promised. She nodded toward Rachel. "And to Shira as well."

"Shira, too, has worked today," said Anna. "She is watching Tobias, which is no small task." She grinned. "But if she receives a portion of this meal, perhaps she will consent to watching him again."

Deborah waved aside the praise. "A meal is little enough wages for the service you have done us."

"My wife speaks the truth." Lappidoth spread his arms wide. "Come, friends. Let us give thanks for this bountiful meal."

They gathered in a circle while Lappidoth spoke the blessing and then seated themselves on the rugs and mats laid out for them. Conversation ceased while everyone filled their empty bellies.

Deborah selected an olive and scanned the circle of friends. Tivon and Adena sat close together, sharing a tray with Ophira, Reuben, Tyrek, and Sabra. From where she sat, they appeared to be three couples enjoying the meal together.

She acknowledged that Tyrek had labored as hard as anyone today, a good sign for a wayward young man, though he wore a sullen pout as he worked. As she watched, he said something to Sabra, who laughed. Deborah frowned. With his troubled past, Tyrek was nearly as unsuitable as Uri, at least until he proved himself committed to a life of honest work and devotion to Yahweh.

Let us receive good news from our relatives. And soon.

"Your worries are written on your face." Dara's comment drew her attention away from the young people. "Is it Asif's accusations?"

Deborah started to deny it but then stopped. The confrontation with Asif had haunted her as she worked. Not his accusations. She was confident in Yahweh's appointment to teach and advise. She glanced sideways, where Lappidoth, Chaim, and Yosef were engaged in conversation as they ate. What bothered her was her husband's longing for peace to return to their home. But that was a conversation she must have with Yahweh, and with Lappidoth himself.

She shook her head. "His accusations are like chaff on the threshing floor. Yahweh's plans for me are the breeze that blows them away." She considered, and then added. "Naturally I would like to be at peace with everyone. Conflict does not honor Yahweh."

"If you are Yahweh's answer to Israel's prayers for a righteous judge to lead us, then there will be peace."

Deborah studied her friend closely. Did she know the role of Israel's judges? She must, for she was a devout woman, one who worshiped Yahweh and knew the history of her people.

"Would Yahweh send a woman into battle?" Deborah asked quietly.

Dara considered the question. "It does seem unlikely," she admitted but then threw up her hands. "Who knows what Yahweh would do? He parted the waters to make a way for our ancestors to escape to freedom. Who would expect that?" She leaned forward to pluck a date off the tray.

Her words calmed a worry that Deborah had not admitted even to herself. Would the people accept a woman as a leader, or would they reject her outright as Asif did? If Yahweh willed it, He would ensure that they accepted her.

Lappidoth lit a lamp, and the flame cast his shadow against the wall in the common room of their house. When he had seated himself on a cushion, Deborah left the worktable and joined him.

The women had helped Deborah store the extra stew and wipe the bowls and platters clean before leaving.

"Yosef said he will come back here to help tomorrow, though Reuben must stay behind and work," he told her. He rested his back against the wall. "If we make as much progress tomorrow, we will finish in three days' time."

"And have a week to spare before Passover." She leaned sideways against him. "We will miss you."

They had decided that Tivon and Sabra would stay behind with her while Lappidoth traveled to Shiloh for Passover. He would have plenty of company among the villagers who also made the pilgrimage.

Sabra entered the house carrying a large jar of goat milk. "I thought I might have to get a second jug tonight. This one is full."

"Where is Tivon?" Lappidoth asked as she made her way carefully to the storeroom.

"He took a lamp into his house to inspect a section of brick that he says is not laid evenly." She ducked into the storeroom.

Lappidoth's chest heaved with a silent laugh. "He worries over that house like a mother over her babes."

"He wants it to be perfect for his bride." Deborah leaned her head on his shoulder. "Did you watch them together tonight? Already they love one another."

"They have known each other from birth," he said. "Many couples do not have that opportunity."

Sabra emerged. She retrieved a cushion and set it on the opposite side of the lamp. "I have dreaded the harvest, but today the work was pleasant."

"Sharing the burden with friends is always more enjoyable than working alone," Deborah said.

"We are blessed to have such neighbors," Lappidoth added.

The girl nodded, her gaze fixed on the flame. "Imma, when the harvest is done, I would like to come with you to the palm tree."

The comment pleased Deborah. Until now Sabra had chosen to stay home and work on her cheese, or even to help her abba at whatever task he performed on their farm.

"As long as you are not needed elsewhere," Deborah said. "What has caused you to change your mind?"

"Talking to Ophira today." She did not look up from the lamp as she spoke. "She says the gathering has grown, and even people from other towns come."

Deborah studied her. It was not the teaching that attracted her but the people? There was something else, something she was not saying.

"That is true," she said. "At times the group is so large my throat burns from talking loudly enough that those farthest away will hear."

Sabra plucked at a loose thread on the cushion. "And people from our village come as well."

Deborah lifted her head from her husband's shoulder. "Many are people we know," she agreed. A thought occurred to her, one that stiffened her spine. "Did Ophira name those from our village?"

Her head tilted sideways. "A few."

"Did she name Uri, perhaps?"

Sabra grew still. "She might have." She swallowed. "Yes, I believe she did."

Deborah set her teeth to trap the hasty words begging to be released. Her concerns about Tyrek fled.

Lappidoth drew a breath and then spoke in an even tone. "Has your imma told you that we will not condone a betrothal with that young man?"

Her head dropped forward so that her face was concealed. "Yes, Abba."

117

Deborah exchanged a long look with Lappidoth. His face reflected her concern. If Sabra harbored feelings for Uri, her young heart would be broken when they arranged a more suitable betrothal.

Still silent, Sabra stood and picked up the cushion. "I am tired," she said, and started toward her bedchamber.

"Sabra."

She stopped at the sound of Deborah's voice but did not turn. Deborah cast about for something to say, something to heal the rift she felt opening between them. No words came.

"May Yahweh bless you with restful sleep," she finally said.

Her answer was a single nod, and then she was gone.

Deborah turned on her cushion to face Lappidoth. "What will we do? I cannot forbid her to learn Torah."

He rubbed a hand across his lips, worry furrowing his brow. "Perhaps I should take her with me to Shiloh. She may be moved by seeing so many devout Israelites gathering at the tabernacle to worship."

Deborah nodded her agreement. "While you are there, Yahweh may reveal the one He has planned for our daughter."

She would not stop praying for that.

CHAPTER ELEVEN

Deborah left her house just before the sixth hour, as was her custom, and cast an eager eye toward the hill. The sight of dozens gathered there sent a thrill coursing through her. In the past few weeks, as Israelites from all over made their way to and from Shiloh for Passover and the Feast of Unleavened Bread, her audience had increased. More often than not, there were more faces she did not recognize than ones she did.

The youngest of the she-goats trotted across the courtyard to stand at her side. Deborah smiled down at the animal, whose sides swelled with an unborn lamb.

"Have no fear for your little one." She rested a hand on the goat's head. "Passover is behind us, at least this year."

With Lappidoth and Sabra gone to Shiloh along with Chaim and Laban and many other friends, Deborah and Tivon had celebrated Passover with Dara, Adena, Levi, Anna, and Tobias. It had been a quiet observance, though the rituals were performed with deep reverence as was fitting and right. Still, the traditions seemed a little emptier without her absent loved ones.

She left the courtyard and climbed the hill, a sense of anticipation swelling with each step. When she sat beneath the palm tree teaching, she felt Yahweh's presence all around her and even inside, pouring His words through her mouth. She sensed His love for those gathered before her, and at times her passion nearly overwhelmed her. Once she became so caught up in the teaching that hours slipped by unnoticed, until the moon made its first appearance in the sky. And yet not one of the listeners left or even commented. It seemed as if Yahweh was pouring Himself out for His people and He had chosen her, the most humble of His children, to be His vessel.

When she neared the top, one person separated himself from the group to approach. Uri, looking smug, as always.

Yahweh, give me patience.

She nodded at the young man and would have passed by, but he stopped her.

"There are Kenites among your listeners today," he told her.

The comment took her by surprise. Not a snide remark intended to rattle her, as he sometimes did, or a criticism on the previous lesson, but an ordinary attempt at conversation.

Kenites, descendants of Jethro, the father-in-law of their deliverer Moses, followed the practices of their ancestors and dwelt in tents, traveling from place to place. Most made their homes in the wide plains in the southern part of Judah, near Arad.

Uri leaned forward. "These two are bound for the north. The man, Heber, tells me their goal is Kedesh."

In spite of herself, the news piqued Deborah's interest. Kedesh lay a great distance to the north, not far from the city where the Canaanite King Jabin dwelt. Reports from recent travelers indicated that attacks by the Canaanite army on

Israelites occurred almost daily in that region. Person after person had expressed to her, "Yahweh must act soon, or Israel will be overrun." Why would anyone wish to travel *to* that location?

Something stirred inside her, so faint she almost did not notice. She had a feeling about these Kenites. Would they somehow play a part in the upcoming conflict?

To Uri she merely nodded and gave a calm reply. "I hope to hear their story before the day is done."

As she moved past him, he took the opportunity to deliver the expected jab, no doubt intended to unnerve her.

"Do you expect Sabra to return soon?"

She stopped and turned. He stood with his arms folded, his lips twisted into what some might take as a smile. He knew full well how it annoyed her to hear her daughter's name on his lips.

Why does this young man take such pleasure in goading me?

Refusing to rise to his attempt, she answered in the same tone as before. "I expect my husband and daughter will be here soon enough."

She left him where he stood and took her place beneath the palm tree.

———————————

For the day's lesson, Deborah had chosen a section from *BaMidbar,* the fourth book of Torah. The holy writ recounted the time when the Hebrew people grumbled against Yahweh, and Moses's failure at the waters of Meribah. The story was one of her favorites. Did not all of them fail Yahweh at one time or another?

As she recited the words recorded in Torah, she scanned her listeners. Some were familiar, though many were strangers. More men than women today. They shared one thing in common. Their intent expressions, the eagerness with which they strained to hear, revealed a hunger for Yahweh that gave her cause to rejoice.

All except two. Near the back of the crowd, to one side and a noticeable distance apart, sat a man and woman. The Kenites Uri mentioned? The man was a hulking figure with a mass of black curls covering his head and face. Though she could not see his features, he sat with his arms folded tightly across his chest, his body leaning backward at an unfriendly angle that implied he wished to distance himself from all around him.

The woman beside him wore a head covering and the heavy robes of a traveler. Her face bore no expression at all.

When Deborah moved from her recitation to outlining the lessons they might learn from their ancestors' actions, all her thoughts focused on Yahweh, and His incredible faithfulness to a people who were unfaithful again and again.

She brought the lesson to a close with the final blessing. "Be strong, be strong, and let us strengthen each other."

A murmur arose as people commented to those seated nearby on the day's message. Deborah stretched her spine and got to her feet, exhaustion creeping over her.

"I see your followers have increased in number since our last visit."

Looking into the man's vaguely familiar face, she searched her memory for his name.

"Shalom, Amram from Hebron." Her gaze included his companions. "Shalom to you all."

His lips broke into a wide smile. "I thought you might have forgotten us."

"Yahweh has blessed me with an able memory," she said. "How was your time in Shiloh?"

"Inspiring." He lifted his hands toward heaven in praise. "The tabernacle, the priests, the ceremonies. And thousands of Israelites gathered before Yahweh to worship. In all my journeys to Shiloh, this was the largest assembly I have ever seen." His hands dropped to his side. "But I heard no teaching as wise as yours."

The man at his side nodded. "We have told everyone we've met about the prophetess who sits beneath a tree and proclaims the word of Yahweh." His gaze trailed upward, to the top of the tree. "It has become known as Deborah's Palm."

Since beginning the Torah teaching, she had heard many such words of praise. She could not take them to heart, for she knew better than any that the wisdom she related came from Yahweh, not from her humble mind.

She answered with a quick smile. "I am honored." Then she turned the subject. "What word is there from the northern tribes? Those who come this way tell of Canaanite attacks that grow more violent by the day."

Amram's expression sobered. "We heard many such tales. We camped beside a company from Jezreel who had suffered heavy losses. Men. Women. Children. Even babes fall victim to

Canaanite swords. Their livestock is stolen or slaughtered, their fields burned." He shook his head, sorrow heavy on his features. "They suffer the destruction of their ancestral land, and many have lost hope."

"The prayer we heard voiced over and over was that Yahweh might raise up a judge in the manner of Shamgar and Ehud," the second man said. Around him heads nodded. "People said surely Yahweh will hear the voices of so many crying out to him."

Amram agreed. "There is a man whose name was on many tongues. Barak son of Abinoam. He lives in Naphtali, in Kedesh."

A tingle erupted deep in Deborah's chest. She grew still, searching inside for the reason. Was it Kedesh? This was the second time in a single day the place had been named in her presence. No, it was the man. Barak son of Abinoam. The tingle spread and became a prickle along her arms.

"Is he a wise man?" she asked.

"I heard no words of praise for his wisdom," Amram said, and his companions agreed. "But he is brave, and passionate to protect his people from harm. It is said he has assembled a band of his kinsmen, armed them with swords and spears, and taught them to fight the Canaanites in their iron chariots."

Amram's friend added, "He has spies situated along the border and tracks the progress of King Jabin's army. At the first sign of a raid, his men rush to meet them in battle."

Deborah's throat had gone dry. "Do you think—" She swallowed and searched Amram's face. "Might he be the one we have prayed for?"

"That was the topic of many a conversation in the camps around the tabernacle." He lifted his gaze. "May Yahweh's will be done."

"Let it be so," she murmured in answer.

Thoughts crowded her mind, each begging for attention. As did the people, those who came to hear her teaching. They gathered all around, waiting until she had finished speaking with the travelers from Hebron so they, too, could talk to her.

She forced herself to focus on them.

"Thank you for stopping here on your way home," she said to Amram and his friends.

"We will camp here a few days, so we can hear more from you." He dipped his head in farewell. "Shalom, wise priestess."

Startled, she could only nod in return. She dared not think what would happen if Asif heard her named as priestess.

When the men moved away, Deborah lifted her head to look at the place the Kenites had occupied. It was empty. Had they left during the teaching or after? She had been so caught up in delivering Yahweh's message, she had not noticed. She had wanted to speak with them, perhaps to further discern their role in Yahweh's incomprehensible plan.

A couple who had waited behind Amram stepped forward, their faces beaming with admiration. Deborah pushed aside thoughts of Kenites, and Kedesh, and Barak, and focused a smile on them.

"Shalom, and welcome. My name is Deborah."

CHAPTER TWELVE

The voice of the woman beneath the palm tree carried across the hilltop and down the slope to where Jael sat, mesmerized. She had not heard the words of Torah since she was a child, growing up in her father's tent in the Wilderness of Zin. Hearing them now, she felt an aching longing in her heart, so powerful she could scarcely draw a breath.

"Then Moses lifted his hand and struck the rock twice with his rod; and water came out abundantly, and the congregation and their animals drank." The teacher paused and drew a deep breath. Jael could not see her eyes from the distance, but when she continued, tears choked her words. "Then Yahweh spoke to Moses and Aaron, 'Because you did not believe Me, to hallow Me in the eyes of the children of Israel, therefore you shall not bring this assembly into the land which I have given them.'"

A gasp went up from the listeners. Glancing sideways, Jael noted that every head faced forward, drawn in by the teacher's words.

All save one.

"I have heard enough," Heber grumbled, his voice low so no one could hear but her. "Come, Wife."

He got to his feet and, without waiting to see if she followed, strode off down the hill in the direction of their camp.

Jael cast a regretful look at the woman teacher. How she longed to stay, to drink in the message that stirred a hunger so intense she feared she might faint if she moved.

But she must. Heber would tolerate nothing less than immediate obedience.

Swallowing against a painful lump that had lodged in her throat, she rose and hurried after her husband.

At the bottom of the hill, he turned west and stalked across a grassy field toward a heavily wooded area some distance away. Jael struggled to keep up with him, taking two steps to each one of his long-legged strides. By the time they reached their camp, her breath labored in her chest. She sank to the ground near the tree where the donkey was tied and watched Heber pace around the area, a scowl heavy on his face. He checked the cart and tested the ropes that held their belongings in place.

Once, early in their marriage, a band of marauders had come upon their camp while they shopped in the marketplace and had stolen his metalwork tools. Even now, years later, Jael shrank at the memory of Heber's rage. Her ties had not been secure enough, nor had the site she selected been secluded enough. Watching him now, she brushed her cheek. The bruises had taken weeks to fade.

"All is well," he announced as he lowered himself to the ground beside her. "Though I had little fear of thievery when I saw the manner of the people gathered on that hillside."

She risked a sideways glance. Over the years she had become adept at judging his mood by the set of his jaw and the shade of his eyes. His lips, barely visible behind the thick beard, bore no sign of tightness. Jael relaxed.

"What manner is that?" she asked.

"Simple. Easily deceived by pretty words and ancient stories." The lips twisted with disdain. "People who are governed by archaic precepts would not dare to offend their god by thieving." The disdain gave way to a grim smile. "Though they would do well to fear my wrath more than an unseen god who does not exist."

She held her tongue. He knew full well she had been raised in a family that revered the Israelite way of life, and their God. At times she wondered if he made such belittling comments as a way to provoke her into voicing an opposing opinion. If so, he would be disappointed. Jael had learned long ago not to disagree with her husband.

"You seemed caught up in the woman's words." His tone held a trace of accusation.

"I remember the passage she recited," Jael answered. She shrugged, as if the memory held no special significance. "The story was one my father told often."

A snort blasted through his nose. "Were he here, he would be up there, fawning over her along with the other fools."

It no longer took much of an effort to maintain a calm demeanor in the face of his insults. She did it many times each day. "I am sure you are right."

"He was a weak-minded fool." He spat the words.

Jael held herself still, aware that he watched to see her reaction. Alarm stiffened her muscles. His mood sometimes turned in an instant, though she had never been able to predict what caused the change. Insults against her or her family often preceded a fit of anger that might leave her bruised or even injured if she did not handle herself with utmost care.

"He was swayed by his own father's teachings, and his father's before him," she said. A neutral statement, neither agreeing nor disagreeing.

"I know that," he snapped. "How often have you boasted that your grandfather's grandfather was the famed Jethro, who gave his daughter to the Hebrew leader Moses?" His words dripped ridicule. "As if that makes you better than your husband."

Fear trailed up her spine like an icy finger. Heber was at his most dangerous when he imagined her thinking highly of herself. She must assure him of her admiration, and quickly.

Turning, she faced him squarely. "How could I boast of such a thing? Jethro was contemptible. Did he not allow the Hebrew to cast his daughter aside, and take her back into his tent?" She gave a scoffing laugh. "As you have said many times, Husband, he was a fool, and taught his sons and grandsons to be the same. It is shame I feel, not pride."

Forgive me, Father, Grandfather.

The fearsome shadows in his eyes lightened the slightest bit. Encouraged, she changed her tone, infusing her words with the merest touch of flattery.

"But now, I do have a reason for pride. In my husband." She held his gaze and let him see the false sincerity in hers. "You will be a mighty ally for King Jabin of Canaan. With your knowledge of the Israelites, he cannot help but see the value in partnering with you." Leaning closer, she lowered her voice. "When we reach Kedesh, I have no doubt you will become one of the king's most trusted advisers."

His chest swelled, and the tight line of his lips curled with pleasure. "When I partner with the Canaanite king, we will be rich."

"I am the most fortunate of wives," she told him.

A different darkness crept over his eyes, one she knew well and dreaded nearly as much as his cruelty. But this torture at least would not leave her maimed.

"Come to me, Wife."

His demand rumbled with lust. Swallowing the sudden rush of bitter bile that rose in her throat, Jael obeyed.

CHAPTER THIRTEEN

Deborah served a small evening meal to Tivon. In Lappidoth and Sabra's absence, they had fallen into a routine. They ate beneath the olive trees to enjoy the abundance of blossoms, which were early this year, no doubt because of the unusually warm weather. When the meal ended, Tivon worked on his house while Deborah settled any tasks that needed handling before returning to the palm tree to pray about the next day's teaching.

Her prayers this evening took a different path.

"Blessed are You Yahweh, King of the universe." She looked up, noting the moon visible in the still light sky. "Twice today You touched my spirit."

The first had been when she heard Uri's words. A chuckle rumbled in her throat. Would that young man not be shocked to learn how his words stirred in her soul? Not taunts about Sabra, but his words about a Kenite journeying northward.

"Does this Kenite worship You?"

That would not be unusual, for Kenites shared a common history with the people of Yahweh. In the generations since the time of Moses and his Kenite father-in-law, the two peoples had dwelt side by side in peace. The nomadic tent dwellers spread across the Wilderness of Zin in the southernmost part of Judah. Why, then, was the couple who attended the teaching today traveling north, into certain danger from Canaanite raiders?

As she pondered the mystery, she sensed something she could not decipher. She did not believe the Kenite couple worshiped the God of Abraham, Isaac, and Jacob. Still, she felt certain they had a role to play in the coming conflict, though they did not know it.

She turned her thoughts instead to Barak son of Abinoam. Once again, a thrill raced through her, and the hair on her arms rose. Barak, who lived in Kedesh, near the palace of the Canaanite king. Barak, who had gathered a group of Israelites to defend Israelites from attacks by Jabin's soldiers.

The words of the men from Hebron, spoken to her on their northbound journey returned to her. *"Your wisdom stands alongside that of Othniel, Ehud, and Shamgar."*

"Yahweh," she whispered, "I have no wisdom, no knowledge, save what You give me."

Her thoughts turned to the judges, beloved by the people not only for their wisdom but also for their courage in battle. Othniel, who had captured the town of Debir and delivered the people from their oppression by the Mesopotamian king, Cushan-Rishathaim. Ehud, who killed Eglan, the king of Moab, and led Israel in eighty years of peace. Shamgar, who killed six hundred Philistines with an oxgoad. Was she, a woman, to claim the title held by such mighty warriors?

"I am no judge, Yahweh. But perhaps this Barak is?"

"Is he a wise man?" she had asked Amram.

He answered, "*I heard no words of praise for his wisdom, but he is brave, and passionate to protect his people from harm.*"

And his companion's words: "*We have told everyone we've met about the prophetess who sits beneath a tree and proclaims the word of Yahweh.*"

"Prophetess."

She laughed quietly to herself, but in the next moment her laughter died. Yahweh had blessed her with a sound memory, and the skill to teach, and with His wisdom. Yahweh had similarly blessed Barak with passion and bravery in battle.

The vision of the stars rose before her again, so vivid her surroundings faded. The children of Israel, each brilliant by themselves. But combined—

She leaped to her feet as Yahweh's plan opened before her like a scroll being unrolled. And like a holy scroll, she gazed in wonder at the wisdom, the magnificence of the contents. Barak *would* lead the army that would deliver the people from the tyranny of King Jabin. But he did not know it.

Yahweh had assigned her, Deborah, to tell him.

Excitement gripped her so that she could not keep her feet still. She danced around the palm tree, joy bubbling in her soul until she could not contain it. A song burst from her, a song of triumph and of praise.

"Hear this, you kings! Listen, you rulers!
You will not stand against the house of Israel.
I, Deborah, will sing to the Lord.
I will praise Yahweh, the God of Israel, in song.
Mountains quake before You, Yahweh.

The seas shout Your praises.
All that You have made with Your hands rejoice."

The song ended. Deborah sank to her knees and lifted her hands to the heavens. Awestruck by His grandeur, His greatness, His majesty, she worshiped.

———————

Night was moments away when she descended the hill, still exhilarated but tired. Bed would feel good tonight. She opened the gate, listening to the sounds of Tivon tapping a brick into place.

"Imma!"

Deborah turned to see Sabra running toward her, and Lappidoth leading the donkey just behind her. Happiness welled up inside her, different from the powerful emotion she experienced on the hill but no less joyful. She caught her daughter in her arms and hugged her tight, noting that the girl's head was nearly of a height with hers.

"How can you have grown nearly a handspan in only a few weeks?" Deborah pushed her to arm's length, her smile so wide her cheeks hurt. She cupped the girl's face with a gentle hand and said tenderly, "My beautiful girl. How I have missed you."

"I have missed you too." With one more quick hug, Sabra released Deborah and dashed away. "Tivon! Come and look what we brought you."

Deborah closed the distance between her and Lappidoth and gathered him in her arms, though this embrace was more tender than the other. His arms pulled her close, and she relished the feel of his strength encircling her.

"Did you miss me as well?" Humor lightened his words.

She leaned back enough to grin into his face. "I might have, once or twice."

Together they led the donkey to the house and untied the ropes holding several large bundles on its back. Once released, the creature heaved a whistling sigh, as though of satisfaction, and trotted across the courtyard to munch on the fresh hay Tivon had placed there for the goats.

"How was your time in Shiloh?" she asked.

He hefted a large bundle onto his shoulder and headed for the house. After selecting a smaller one, Deborah followed.

"It was good," he said. "The biggest gathering in many years, I would say."

"I have heard the same report from others." She entered the courtyard. "To what do you attribute the increase?"

"The Canaanites," he said without hesitation. "I could not count the number I met from the northern tribes. Issachar, Zebulun, Naphtali. Even Asher. All those who suffer at the hands of the Canaanite army. And the tales they tell." He shook his head, sorrow etched on his features.

They entered the house, and Deborah instructed him to set his burden on the worktable, where she would unpack it.

"I am not sure I wish to hear them," she said.

"No more than I wish to repeat them." He took a cup from a shelf and filled it with water from the jug.

She untied a knot and opened the canvas wrapping. Soiled clothing from their trip. Tomorrow she would send Sabra to the stream.

"Did you meet anyone with a son that might become our daughter's husband?" she asked.

A defeated sigh escaped his lips. "I met many young men, but none of them seemed right to me. Fine men in their ways," he added, "but not for our Sabra."

"Is it possible that you ask too much of the man who will take your daughter from you?" Her lips twitched with humor.

Instead of replying, he downed the water and replaced the cup. They would have to discuss the matter soon, but for now Deborah found it difficult to think of anything except the plan Yahweh had revealed to her.

"I have had many visitors at the palm tree as people from the southern tribes return to their homes," she told him. Watching closely for his reaction, she asked, "Did you hear of a man from Naphtali named Barak son of Abinoam?"

"Hear of him?" His chest heaved with a silent laugh. "The man's name was on every tongue. Not a day passed without someone extoling his virtues, his bravery." He joined her at the worktable. "What did you hear of him?"

"The same." She set the washing to one side and reached for the larger bundle. "Lappidoth, I—"

"I gave Tivon the bangles," Sabra announced as she burst into the house. "He was pleased and says they will make a fine addition to his *mattan*, and Adena will cherish them."

"As we knew he would be." Lappidoth and Sabra exchanged a smile. "And?"

Grinning, she reached into a pouch hanging at her side. Metal clanged against metal as she withdrew her hand. "We got these for you, Imma."

Deborah took the gift, a trio of silver bracelets. The thickest one had been embellished, and she examined the design etched in the surface.

"They are palm trees." Delighted, she looked up to find Lappidoth watching her, pleasure plain on his features.

"Barak's was not the only name we heard often in Shiloh," he told her. "Word also spread of a wise woman from Ephraim who teaches Torah with authority. They say she sits beneath a tree, Deborah's Palm." He nodded toward the bracelet. "Hence the design."

"The silversmith and his family pitched their tent near ours." Sabra looked at Lappidoth and pulled a frown. "Abba would not let me tell him that Deborah is my own imma."

Deborah fingered the etching. "Then how did—"

"Laban," Lappidoth said. "The boy would not hold his tongue, no matter how sternly Chaim and I spoke to him."

Slipping the bracelets onto her wrist, she looked from daughter to husband. "Thank you. I shall treasure these gifts."

Looking satisfied, Sabra glanced toward the storeroom. "Is there any bread? We had nothing but a light meal this evening because Abba was eager to get home."

"There is." Deborah placed a hand on the bundle they had not yet unpacked. "If you two will see to this, I will prepare food for my hungry travelers."

She headed for the storeroom. Her conversation with Lappidoth would have to wait. Though she wasn't sure she could hold her tongue for long.

That night, as she lay curled up against her husband on their bedstead, Deborah knew the time had come.

"What is it?" Lappidoth asked before she opened her mouth.

She drew back to look him in the eye. "What do you mean?"

A tender smile curved his lips. "After more than twenty years, I know my wife. Something has happened to worry you, and you wish to tell me about it."

"I am not worried," she said quickly. "But I do have something to discuss with you."

Throughout the evening as she had planned what she would say, she remembered that she had not mentioned her vision in the stars, though that had been many weeks ago. She sat up on the bed beside him so she could spread her arms wide as she described the greatness, the vastness of the blazing image in the skies.

"And then, just today, I learned the deeper meaning of the vision." She recounted her conversation with Amram and the tingling certainty she felt when he mentioned the name of

Barak. Words tumbled from her mouth as she recalled her confession to Yahweh, that she was not a mighty warrior like Ehud and the rest. And her amazement when He revealed the details of His plan.

When she ran out of words, she fell silent. Lappidoth, still on his back with his arms behind his head, stared at the dark ceiling above the bedstead. Try though she might, she could read nothing in his expression.

Finally, she could stand it no more. "Well? What have you to say?"

His lips pursed. "First, I am glad you do not intend to run off to battle the Canaanites." He glanced at her. "I confess the idea that you might has occurred to me once or twice."

She did not want to admit that the thought had lurked at the back of her mind for weeks. She gave a weak laugh. "I can barely lift the stewpot when it is full. How could I wield a sword?"

He acknowledged the comment with a faint smile that disappeared as quickly as it arrived. "My second thought is that you must do as Yahweh commands. You must send a message to Barak in Naphtali and tell him what Yahweh has shown you."

Her shoulders wilted as tension fled. He believed her. "Thank you. That is what I felt I must do as well."

He shifted on the mat and rose to sit cross-legged facing her. "My final thought is one of disappointment that you did not trust me enough to tell me of the vision. Did you fear I would not believe you, or that I would dissuade you from giving whatever Yahweh asks of you? Of *us*?"

The hurt she saw in his eyes stabbed her heart like a blade. "It was not that," she whispered, willing him to believe her. "If I had any doubts, they were about myself. Never about you."

He cupped her face in both of his hands, his palms warm against her cheeks. "I am your husband. You can trust me with anything. And I vow that I will always believe in you, my Deborah."

Tears of relief, and of joy, filled her eyes in the moment before he pulled her close for a kiss.

CHAPTER FOURTEEN

D eborah woke early the next morning and was up before
the sun. Her sleep had been fitful, and several times she
started awake, words of the message she must write filling her
mind. She hurried through her morning task of preparing a
meal for her family and then set it aside, ready to be eaten.

From the storeroom she fetched a thick leather pouch containing the wax tablets she had used to teach Tivon and Sabra
reading and writing. From the bottom of the pouch, she drew
out a wooden tube containing a scroll of papyrus. She had
obtained it several years ago in Shiloh during one of the pilgrimage festivals. At the time, she had not been sure why she
felt the urge to purchase such a costly item. Tablets could be
purchased inexpensively and had served her well for teaching
and sending the occasional message to her family. But the message she must send now could not be trusted to wax, which
might easily be damaged and rendered unreadable on the
long journey to Kedesh.

She scooped a quantity of ash from the cooking fire and
mixed it with oil. Since she had no pitch, she added a bit of thick-
ened honey and formed an unspoken prayer that her ink would
remain legible. When the mixture was the right consistency, she
filled a hollow reed stylus, unrolled the scroll, and began.

Lappidoth emerged from their bedchamber as she wrote the last word.

"You have wasted no time," he said, coming to stand behind her at the worktable. "May I read the message?"

She set her reed down and moved aside, inviting him closer.

Deborah, wife of Lappidoth, who dwells in the village south of Bethel in Ephraim, sends greetings to Barak son of Abinoam, who dwells in Naphtali the town of Kedesh. Yahweh has heard the cries of His people. I have seen a vision in the stars. You are Yahweh's chosen instrument to bring an end to the brutality of the Canaanites. Make haste to Deborah's Palm.

He nodded. "There is but one thing left."

Concerned, she glanced at the papyrus. "What have I left unsaid?"

"Nothing. The message is clear and compelling." The beloved lopsided grin twisted his lips. "The thing we must do now is inform our daughter that she must vacate her bedchamber to make room for our honored guest."

Relieved, Deborah returned the grin. "That and hire a messenger to travel north." She sobered. "There are not many who will willingly venture into the territory where Canaanite attacks occur often."

He lifted a shoulder, unconcerned. "It is Yahweh's message. He will see it delivered into Barak's hands."

Reassured, Deborah could only agree.

Midmorning found Deborah kneeling in the vegetable garden, mounding soil around the tender leek stalks. She sang as she worked, the song that Moses and the children of Israel sang when Yahweh delivered them from slavery in Egypt.

"I will sing unto Yahweh, for he hath triumphed gloriously: the horse and his rider hath he thrown into the sea."

A noise from behind pulled her from the song. Turning, she saw a woman standing at the corner of the courtyard wall.

Deborah sat back on her heels. "Shalom."

The woman started, then nodded, and finally answered in an almost inaudible voice. "Shalom."

Deborah stood and, dusting the dirt from her hands, moved closer. "I am Deborah."

The woman gave a quick nod and remained silent. She did not meet Deborah's eyes but kept her head down, her face nearly concealed by a thick head covering. Was she bashful? She held herself stiff, her arms pulled close to her body, her shoulders rigid beneath a heavy traveling robe. Not bashful, Deborah decided, but fearful.

Yahweh, how can I help this woman?

Speaking in a low, pleasant voice, she asked, "May I know your name?"

After a pause, she answered, "I am Jael."

"Welcome, Jael." Deborah waved at the vegetable plot behind her. "What good fortune that you arrived as I was finishing my work. Please come inside and join me for something cool to drink and perhaps a fig cake."

Jael shook her head in a quick, jerky movement. "I must get back quickly, before—"

Deborah itched to question her, to know what she must return to. Was that what frightened her so?

"I see," she said. "What can I do for you?"

"I—" Jael lifted her head and pushed back her head covering. "I came to ask a question."

Looking upon her face, Deborah realized she had seen the woman before. Yesterday, on the hill. This was the Kenite woman, the one who, with her husband, traveled north to Kedesh. Deborah had felt a stirring in her spirit when Uri told her their destination.

The very destination to which her message must be taken.

"You came yesterday to the palm tree," she said. "I hoped to speak with you after the teaching but did not see you then. You are traveling to Kedesh?"

Questions appeared in the form of creases on her brow. "Yes, we are."

"Would you deliver a message to a man who lives there?" she asked. "I will gladly pay you."

Jael shook her head. "I am sorry, truly. But I cannot."

"Perhaps your husband, then?"

At the mention of her husband, fear flashed into Jael's eyes. An ache throbbed in Deborah's chest as she realized the reason for the tense posture, the hunched shoulders. She had known a few unfortunate women bound to cruel husbands.

Yahweh, what can I do?

"Please allow me to show you hospitality," she said softly. "I would like to know you better."

Jael's lips pressed tight, and again she shook her head. "I have only a short time, but I want to ask you…"

"Yes?" Deborah prompted.

"Does your God punish those who do not follow the mitzvah of your holy writings? The writings you teach beneath your palm tree."

The question took Deborah by surprise, though she took pains to hide it. This woman, this Kenite, feared the wrath of Yahweh?

For a long moment she made no answer. Not until she knew the words she spoke came from a wiser Source than she.

"Yahweh gave the mitzvah to the children of Abraham, Isaac, and Jacob. We who are their descendants are bound by a holy covenant. Those of other ancestry are not."

Jael considered the answer and gave a slow nod.

Deborah added, "Yahweh does punish outsiders but only when they harm His people, the children of Israel."

Jael's eyes went round, and all color faded from her face. She wavered on her feet as though she might fall. Deborah reached out a hand to steady her, but Jael jerked away from her hand.

"I am sorry," Deborah told her. "I did not mean to upset you."

Tears welled in Jael's eyes. "What if…" She swallowed, and then shook her head.

"Yahweh is just," Deborah said, "but He is also merciful. He instructs us to show kindness to the poor and needy, even those who are not children of the covenant. And He makes provisions for those who wish to enter into the covenant."

Jael blinked away her tears and fixed her eyes on Deborah, listening closely.

Encouraged, Deborah went on. "In the third book of Torah, *Vayikra*, it is written: 'The stranger that dwells with you shall be unto you as one born among you, and you shalt love him as yourself, for you were strangers in the land of Egypt. I am Yahweh, your Elohim.'"

The words from Torah hung in the air between them, resonating as if they were living things. Deborah's flesh tingled. She had meant the passage to soothe Jael's fears, but Yahweh had delivered a message. Deborah did not know why, but she knew those words would one day bring about His plan in Jael's life.

"Thank you," Jael whispered. She took a backward step. "I must go."

Pulling her head covering over her head, she turned and started to leave.

"Wait."

Jael stopped. She half turned to lift a questioning gaze.

Deborah raised her hand, palm toward Jael, and bestowed a blessing. "May Yahweh guide your footsteps toward peace. May He rescue you from the hand of every foe. May He bless your handiwork, and grant you grace, kindness, and mercy in His eyes and the eyes of all who see you. And may He give you peace."

A smile, small and shadowy but genuine, crept over Jael's lips. She dipped her head once, whether in agreement or farewell Deborah did not know. And then she was gone.

As Deborah returned to the vegetables, an insight settled on her, a certainty she could not explain. Somehow, she would hear of Jael again.

CHAPTER FIFTEEN

At the sixth hour, Debora left her house for her teaching beneath the palm tree. She had dispatched Tivon to the village to inquire about a courier to take her message to Kedesh. Outside the courtyard wall, she shielded her eyes and looked in that direction. No sign of Tivon. Instead, she spied Ophira hurrying toward her.

"Shalom, Ophira," she called when the young woman neared.

Ophira broke into a run. The next instant she flung herself into Deborah's arms and sobbed onto her shoulder. Concerned, Deborah held her close and let her cry.

When her tearful heaves stilled, she pulled back enough to look into Deborah's face. The skin around her eyes was red and swollen, her nose raw.

"It is Tyrek." She drew in a shuddering breath. "He is gone."

"Has he returned home to Jericho?"

She shook her head. "His belongings are still at the house, in the room he shares with Reuben's brothers. They say his pallet remained empty all night." Her face crumpled with a new onslaught of tears. "I fear he has come to harm. Perhaps he encountered Canaanites intent on raiding our village and tried to stop them. Or he might have gone into the woods and been injured by a wild animal, or fell into a pit, or—"

Deborah placed a finger over the girl's lips. "Or perhaps he decided to return home and was ashamed to tell you or Yosef."

She shook her head, rubbing her wet cheeks. "Abba would not allow him to return. He knows that."

"Are there others he might go to? Cousins, perhaps, or uncles?"

"No." She spoke with certainty. "There is no one. And if he intended to leave, would he not have taken his clothing, his personal items? Something terrible has happened, I know it."

The sobs returned, and she would have fallen to the ground had Deborah not pulled her close again.

You know all things, Yahweh. Is Tyrek injured? Has he been killed?

She searched her soul for Yahweh's answer. A great sorrow arose, as if the King of the universe mourned for the young man. Deborah closed her eyes, her heart aching. Not because Tyrek had been killed. He lived still, of that she was certain. Yahweh grieved for Tyrek as a mother would ache for her sick child.

"He is not dead," she told Ophira.

The younger woman pulled back and searched Deborah's face. A flicker of hope appeared in her reddened eyes.

"Then what—"

Deborah shook her head. "I do not know where he is, or what has happened to him, only that he lives. Cling to that and commit him to Yahweh. Besides"—Deborah smiled—"your concern must now lie chiefly with another, should it not?"

When Ophira looked uncertain, Deborah placed a hand against her belly. "Your babe wants his imma to be happy."

Ophira's mouth gaped open. "How did you know?" She shot an awed glance toward heaven.

Deborah laughed. "No, Yahweh did not tell me. When I held you close, I felt the swelling of the babe you carry."

The young woman's hands spread across her belly in the manner of protective mothers everywhere. A hesitant smile appeared on her face. "My heart overflows with gratitude to Yahweh for showing me His favor. I have told no one but Reuben."

"Soon you will not need to tell anyone. The babe will make himself known as he grows." Deborah drew her again into a quick embrace. "Tivon has gone to the village on an errand. Find him, and tell him I give him leave to join the search for your brother."

Ophira's eyes shut as fear for her brother's safety returned. "Thank you." She turned to go but then stopped. She faced Deborah again. "You said *he*. Has Yahweh told you I will bear a son?"

Chuckling, Deborah shook her head. "I name all unborn babes *he,* until she arrives and proves me otherwise."

They parted, and Deborah continued up the hill. When she reached the palm tree, she came to an abrupt halt. Dozens gathered before her, as always, waiting to be taught from Torah. Uri also was there, seated in his usual place near the front and wearing a wide grin. Deborah ignored him. She could not take her gaze from the girl sitting a short distance away from him.

She marched up to Sabra, aware that all eyes were fixed on her. With an effort, she maintained a tranquil expression.

"Were you not helping your abba tend to barley sheaves today?"

Sabra jumped to her feet. "I was, but he gave me leave to come and hear today's teaching."

Color rode high on her cheeks as she returned Deborah's gaze. With a start Deborah realized her recent growth put them on level with each other. Though not yet fully a woman, she was no longer a girl.

From the corner of her eye, she saw Uri peering at them. Likewise, all talk in the immediate area had ceased as the curious people watched.

How can I teach with the idolator's son seated near my daughter? Yahweh, I need Your help!

A sense of calm came over her. Again, her inner being resonated with Yahweh's answer.

Trust.

Did she trust the King of the universe with Sabra's future, her well-being? The question was not worth asking, even of herself. Trust Him she must, for without Yahweh her life would be nothing. She would crumble to dust.

Lifting her voice, she addressed those gathered before her. "Today I am blessed, for my daughter has come to hear the words of Torah."

A murmur of approval swept through those assembled. Sabra's rigid posture relaxed, and her lips—when had they become so plump and lovely?—broke into a smile.

She turned and approached the tree. With her back to her listeners, she placed a hand on the trunk and closed her eyes.

The bark felt rough and prickled her fingers. In her mind, she repeated her daily prayer.

Yahweh, give me Your words, Your wisdom.

Not until she felt Yahweh's shalom settle on her did she turn and face the gathering.

"Let us begin with a blessing."

As always, people came forward at the end of her teaching to speak with her. Some questioned her concerning Torah, while others sought her advice. Deborah gave each one her attention and bestowed blessings before they parted. When the last one left, weariness tugged at her limbs, her eyelids. If she hurried home, she could rest for a few moments before beginning her preparations for the family's evening meal.

Her gaze fell on Sabra, still seated in the same place. As was Uri. The distance between them remained proper, though they now sat facing one another. Sabra's hands sketched an invisible design in the air as she spoke, and Uri nodded in response.

Expelling her irritation in a loud breath, Deborah approached the pair. "Come, Sabra. We must go."

She had not intended her voice to sound so sharp. The hurt in the eyes Sabra lifted to hers stung Deborah's heart.

"Tonight's will be the first meal we have prepared together since your journey to the tabernacle," she added in a calmer tone.

Sabra stood, her head bowed, and together they started down the hill.

"Sabra."

They both turned at Uri's voice.

"Shalom," he said.

A shy smile curved her lips. "Shalom to you."

His gaze switched to Deborah, and his mouth twisted. "And to you, Teacher."

Instead of answering, Deborah inclined her head before turning away.

They walked in silence most of the way. Questions crowded Deborah's mind, but she held her tongue until they neared the beehives. She stepped closer to inspect the first. A steady stream of bees entered and left through the opening in the end of the clay cylinders. The activity assured her that the bees were healthy and hard at work.

"What did you and Uri talk about?" she asked without looking in Sabra's direction.

"He asked about our pilgrimage."

Deborah moved to the next hive. "What did you tell him?"

"I described the tents spreading out from the tabernacle in all directions, as far as I could see, and the merchants selling wares we never have in our village, and the evenings gathered around firepits with people from all over Israel. And about the sacrifices the priests made." When she paused, Deborah glanced up to find a grimace on her face. "I know we have made the pilgrimage before, but I did not remember the smell of blood and burning flesh."

Deborah knew them well. "What always stands out to me are the sounds. So many people and animals crowded into one

153

place, each eager to present their offering at Yahweh's tabernacle. Sometimes my ears grow numb."

Sabra nodded, and Deborah moved to the third hive. The lid that allowed her access to the honeycomb sat crooked. She adjusted it, careful not to disturb the bees inside.

"Uri was truly interested," Sabra said. "I think he would like to go at *Shavuot*."

Deborah straightened abruptly. "Did he tell you this?"

Sabra avoided her gaze. "No, but he asked so many questions I think he was interested."

The idea struck Deborah as unlikely. In her dealings with Uri, he delivered every question as though it were a trap he wished to spring on her.

Turning back to the hive, Deborah adjusted the lid once more. Satisfied that it was in place, she stepped away. Without looking at Sabra, she asked a question.

"Do you remember when you were younger and came here with me? You thought the bees were lovely and set about trying to catch one while my back was turned."

"How could I forget? Even now my hand stings at the memory."

"Do you remember what you asked me?" She looked up to find Sabra shaking her head. "You asked how a creature that was so beautiful and produced something so sweet could also hurt so badly."

Watching, Deborah saw the moment when understanding dawned in Sabra's eyes.

"Come," she said. "I wish to prepare a special meal to welcome you and your abba home."

Tivon did not return until their evening meal neared the end. Seated on the roof with Lappidoth and Sabra, Deborah caught sight of him when he topped a swell in the land.

"Your son is home," she told Lappidoth as she stood. "I will help him wash so he may join us."

He leaned his head back and raised his eyebrows in her direction. Chuckling, she realized she could not fool her husband.

"Yes, I am eager to hear his news," she admitted before descending the stairs.

She met Tivon at the courtyard gate and blurted her question. "Did you find a messenger?"

"I did," he said. "Samuel and his son leave tomorrow for Issachar with a load of woolen fabric for trade. He agreed to extend the journey northward to Kedesh. For a hefty price," he added with a scowl.

Samuel. Deborah would not have entrusted the wool merchant with such an important message. Since his father rested with his ancestors some years ago, he had fallen away from the teachings of Moses. But surely the timing could not be by chance. Yahweh would see the scroll delivered into Barak's hands.

"Thank you," she told her son. "Did you join in the search for Tyrek?"

Disgust twisted his lips. "He has been found, along with a half-dozen empty wineskins, stolen from Yosef's storeroom. He lay in a drunken stupor in a cave in the woods to the west of the village."

Sorrow squeezed Deborah's heart. Ophira must be shocked. No, not shocked. Embarrassed before Reuben's family and humiliated before the entire village for sounding a false alarm.

"He is a troubled young man," she told Tivon. "My heart aches for his family."

"Troubled?" He snorted, his dislike apparent. "*Trouble* is more fitting. Reuben, Yosef, and I wasted hours searching for him, and when Uri dragged him home stinking of sour wine and unable to stand upright, not a word of thanks did he utter."

Deborah stiffened. "Uri found him?"

"It seems that cave is frequented by those who seek a place to indulge in riotous living." Tivon folded his arms. "I have never heard of it, but it is known to Uri." He rubbed his stomach. "Enough about Tyrek. I hope there is something to eat. I am as hungry as a wolf." He opened the courtyard gate and disappeared into the house.

Deborah stayed where she was, thinking over what he had said. A cave in the woods where wayward young men went to indulge in activities of which their parents would not approve. How often had Uri visited the place himself? It came as no surprise that he had been aware of this cave.

As she followed her son into the house, she spared a grateful thought that Tivon had not.

CHAPTER SIXTEEN

Deborah waited for a reply to her message, counting each day with increasing impatience. When she heard that Samuel and his son had returned from their journey, she visited them at their sheep farm, which lay to the east of the village and bordered that of Gersham and his sons. Samuel assured her that they had traveled north to Kedesh, found the home of Barak, and delivered the scroll.

"Did you place it in his hands?" Deborah asked. "Did he read it?"

"He was not there," Samuel answered. "His brother told us he had taken a few of his men to Hazor."

Her breath came shallow in her chest. Tivon had paid him a generous amount to deliver the message into Barak's hands. "You left the scroll with his brother?"

Samuel sat on a bench, a carding comb on his knees. As they talked, he drew a handful of wool through the iron teeth of the comb. When he had untangled a handful, he set those fibers aside and reached for another.

"He was not expected for several days," he told Deborah. "We had already extended our journey by several days and could not spare more to wait for him." He examined the untangled fibers and, apparently satisfied, set them aside and reached for another knotted handful. He sounded annoyed when he peered up at her and asked, "What would you have had me do? Bring your message home with us?"

"No," she answered quickly. "No, what you did was right."

With a nod, he began carding the tangled wool. "The man seemed trustworthy. He will see your message delivered."

After thanking him, Deborah returned home, praying the whole way that Yahweh would safeguard that scroll and see it delivered to Barak.

Another week passed. From the vantage point of her palm tree, she scanned the landscape to the north several times each day, waiting for Barak's approach.

She voiced her concern to Lappidoth. "What if his brother forgot? Or what if Barak read the message but discounted it as foolish?"

"An invitation to visit Deborah the prophetess?" her husband teased. "How could any sane man refuse?"

Seeing his lips twitch with humor, she gave him a playful shove. He caught her hand and placed a kiss in her palm.

"Is the message yours, or Yahweh's?" he asked.

His meaning became clear at once. She had been directed to contact the man by the King of the universe. Yahweh would certainly see His message delivered.

"Thank you," she told her husband.

Barak arrived the following day.

Deborah was in the courtyard, stirring a pot of beeswax suspended over hot coals. Beside her lay a pile of tightly braided fibers ready to dip. She was so absorbed in watching the wax and testing its consistency that she did not hear anything until Lappidoth spoke.

"Deborah. You have a visitor."

She looked up to find him and a stranger standing just beyond the courtyard wall. The instant she saw him, she knew who he was.

Barak was a huge man, standing a full head taller than Lappidoth. His shoulders were broad, and muscles bulged on his bare arms. He wore his black hair pulled back and secured with a thin strip of leather, and his skin gleamed, bronzed from the sun. In a glance she took in the pack slung across one shoulder and the sword that protruded from it. He peered at her with eyes as black as the sky on a moonless night, eyes that sparked with intelligence.

A sense of awe stole over her. She was looking at the man Yahweh had chosen to save His children from persecution by the Canaanites.

She grabbed a folded cloth and moved the pot from the coals before standing.

"Shalom," she said, pleased when the word came out strong. "I am Deborah."

"Shalom, Deborah. I am Barak." He inclined his head in a greeting. "I received your message and have come, as you requested."

"I welcome you as a guest in my home." She glanced at Lappidoth and corrected herself. "In our home."

With a grin, Lappidoth opened the courtyard gate and gestured toward the house. "Be welcome, Barak from Naphtali. Our home is your home."

When Barak entered the courtyard, Lappidoth caught Deborah's eye behind his back and winked. The private message put her immediately at ease. With a grateful glance at her husband, she led the way into the house.

Inside, she led Barak to Sabra's bedchamber. She circled the room, gathering Sabra's belongings.

"This room will be yours for as long as you are with us," she told him, snatching a dress from the pegs on the wall.

His gaze circled the room. After crossing to an alcove in the wall, he picked up a pendant. "Your daughter's?" When Deborah nodded, he said, "I met her when I arrived, and your son as well. They were working with your husband in the field. I would not want to inconvenience either of them. I can sleep on the roof."

Deborah dismissed his suggestion. "You are our guest."

He cocked his head and told her in an amused tone, "When my men and I are guarding against an attack, I am accustomed to resting my head wherever I find myself when sleep overtakes me. On the grass, or even rocky ground."

"That may be, but in my house you will sleep on a bed." Realizing she sounded like a scolding mother, she smiled to soften the words. "I will bring water so that you may refresh yourself after your journey. And then, when you are ready, we will talk."

His eyes pierced hers. "We have much to discuss."

With a nod, she left the room, her arms full of Sabra's things.

She found Lappidoth leaning against the worktable, waiting for her. Motioning for him to follow her, she led him into their bedchamber.

"He has the build of a warrior," she whispered. "The moment I saw him I knew he could be none other than Yahweh's chosen."

"He is a powerful man," Lappidoth agreed. "But more importantly, his devotion to Yahweh is strong. We spoke on the short walk from the field, and he told me a little of his efforts in the north. He is driven by his passion to guard the people of Naphtali against abuse by Canaanite soldiers."

"That is good." She deposited her load in the corner and turned to face him. "He will need power, strength, and passion if he hopes to accomplish the task he has been given."

Since custom prohibited a woman from being left alone with a man to whom she was not married—even Yahweh's hand-picked commander—Barak left the house with Lappidoth to check on Sabra and Tivon in the field. Soon after, Sabra returned home.

"They sent me to help you." She joined Deborah at the worktable. "Barak is a huge man." Her eyes were round as ripe pomegranates.

"I noticed." Deborah cut a slice of melon and laid it on a platter.

"When he spoke, his voice was so deep." Sabra added, "But not gruff. He spoke kindly to me."

Deborah hid a smile. Her daughter was clearly impressed with their visitor from Naphtali. If his presence served to remind her that Uri was not the only handsome man in Israel, so much the better.

"Why is he here?" Sabra asked. "We did not meet him in Shiloh."

Lappidoth had deemed it best not to tell either of their children of Deborah's vision. Since Deborah herself was unsure of the manner in which Yahweh would reveal His plan, she readily agreed.

"He mentioned hearing of Deborah's Palm," she said in answer. "I think he wants to see if there is truth behind the rumors of a woman teacher of Torah."

Sabra plucked a slice of melon from the platter and bit into it. "If his visit means we have melon with our meals, I hope he stays a long time." Grinning, she wiped juice from her chin.

Returning the smile, Deborah instructed, "Go out to the vegetable garden and bring me five radishes." Sabra turned to go. "You know how to check that they are ripe?"

In answer, she cast a glance over her shoulder, eyebrows raised. Sabra had been harvesting vegetables since she could walk. At times Deborah's comments came from habit and not necessity. She laughed at herself and waved Sabra on.

When the men arrived, the meal tray was ready. Deborah carried it up the stairs to the roof, Sabra following with water and a wineskin.

Barak's eyes lit when she set the tray before them. "Do you feast like this at every meal?"

Tivon laughed. "Hardly."

Deborah aimed a mock scowl at her son. "You eat well enough."

"Yes, but not like this."

Barak dipped his head and said to Deborah, "I am honored."

"As are we," she answered.

Lappidoth raised his hands and spoke a blessing over the food, then picked up the wineskin and a cup. He extended it toward Barak, who shook his head.

"Only rarely do I drink wine," he said. "In the north, we must keep our wits about us. An attack can come at any time."

Interest flared in Tivon's eyes. "We have seen few Canaanite raids here, but they are vicious. Tell us, have you encountered the iron chariots?"

"Many times." Barak took a cup of water from Sabra with a smile of thanks, which faded when he spoke again. "Our spies tell us that Sisera has eight hundred, and his king has ordered another hundred."

"Sisera?" Deborah asked.

Barak's gaze slid to her. "The commander of King Jabin's army. A shrewd strategist and a savage warrior. I faced him once, and only by the will of Yahweh left the encounter alive." He rubbed a scar on his upper arm absently. "Three of my men were not so fortunate."

Lappidoth asked, "How many men do you have?"

"Less than one hundred."

"And how many men does Sisera command?" Tivon asked.

Barak answered, keeping his gaze locked on Deborah's. "Forty thousand."

"And nine hundred iron chariots," Tivon said quietly, his tone heavy with dread.

Sabra halted in the act of picking up a slice of melon. "If the king sends his army into Israel, how can we survive?" Her voice broke on the last word.

The question sliced through Deborah's thoughts. For the first time, she knew the size of the obstacles before them, and the knowledge left her insides quaking.

Barak broke eye contact to turn a smile on Sabra. "On our own? We cannot. But we are not left alone. We are descendants of Abraham and heirs to the covenant he made. What we cannot accomplish on our own, Yahweh can do with a single breath."

Power rang in his words, and the quaking inside Deborah stilled. He spoke truth. One day soon they would see the power of Yahweh, and His victory would be so mighty the story would resound through the people for ages to come.

She tore a piece of bread and reached for the honey jar. "Let us not plague our guest with talk of armies and battles."

Lappidoth agreed. "Instead, let us enjoy the feast Yahweh has provided. Barak, tonight you will taste the sweetest honey in all of Israel."

"The sweetest in the land of milk and honey?" He held out a hand for the jar. "I am truly honored."

After the meal, Tivon announced his intention to visit his betrothed. Deborah sent a clearly reluctant Sabra with him.

"I am tired," she complained as she helped Deborah store the uneaten portion of the meal. "Why can I not stay here?"

She did not look the least bit tired, but Deborah did not comment on the fact. Instead, she said truthfully, "Because your abba and I wish to talk to our guest alone."

"What will you talk about?" Sabra asked. "Why will you not tell me the reason Barak is here?"

"You will know soon enough." Deborah covered the honey jar with a square of waxed cloth and tied it in place.

"If you let me stay, I will not listen," Sabra insisted, but at a look from Deborah, she lowered her head and heaved a resigned sigh. "I will go with Tivon."

Deborah cupped one of her smooth cheeks in her hand. How she loved this child she had borne. What could rival the love between a mother and her daughter?

The love between the King of the universe and His children.

She did not know if the thought was hers or Yahweh's.

When Tivon and Sabra left the house, she returned to the roof and seated herself facing Barak. From a pouch at his waist, he removed the cylinder containing her message. He removed the scroll and unrolled it.

"You mentioned a vision in the stars," he said. "Tell me."

Closing her eyes, she described the sight Yahweh had shown her. As she spoke, a chill stole over her and the hair on her arms prickled. Again she saw the brilliant light illuminating the heavens. Again the meaning rang in her spirit.

When she opened her eyes, she found Barak staring intently at her face.

"How do you know Yahweh has appointed me?"

How could she describe a feeling, a tingling in her inner being when she first heard his name? No words could describe her conviction, her certainty. To try would lessen the message.

Instead, she held his gaze and said simply, "Yahweh told me."

He rose and began to pace the length of the rooftop. Deborah and Lappidoth exchanged a glance.

"You heard the size of Sisera's army," he said as he strode past them. "I have only one hundred men."

She replied before she knew she was going to speak. "You will command an army of your own."

He whirled to face her. "How many men?"

A number sprouted to life in her mind. "Ten thousand men from the tribes of Naphtali and Zebulun."

"Ten thousand against forty thousand, and nearly a thousand iron chariots?" He shook his head. "We will be slaughtered beneath the wheels of those chariots."

"No!" The shout surprised her, and even more when she found herself on her feet stalking toward him. When they stood toe to toe, she said, "Yahweh has heard the cry of His children. You will not be slaughtered. Neither will you stand alone. A short while ago you told my daughter that Yahweh can defeat this army with a breath. A breath! How much more can He do with ten thousand men devoted to Him under the leadership of the man He has appointed?" A fire blazed in her soul as words poured from her mouth. "What is forty thousand against ten thousand to Yahweh? Did the Edomites not outnumber Othniel's army? Did Ehud not defeat ten thousand Moabite soldiers with men from just one tribe, the tribe of Ephraim? Was not Shamgar outnumbered by six hundred to one? Do not doubt that Yahweh will rule the day that the children of Israel meet the Canaanites."

When the flow of words ceased, Deborah stood still, holding his gaze, her breath heaving in her chest.

Barak was the first to look away. He walked to the edge of the rooftop and stood beside the low protective wall and gazed out over the land. Deborah returned to her mat. Lappidoth reached over to take her hand. She squeezed his tightly, comforted by the confidence she saw in his face.

Finally, Barak turned. "Since I read your message, I have felt..." He shook his head. "I cannot describe the feelings. Joy that Yahweh has not forgotten us and confidence that He will win the day, whenever that day comes. And may it be soon, before too many more of our people have fallen victim to Sisera's cruelty."

He lifted his face to the sky, where a few stars twinkled in the waning light. Deborah watched him, impatient for his answer.

"I must think," he said.

Hope deflated, and her shoulders sagged. She so hoped, even expected, he would embrace Yahweh's vision immediately, as she had.

"And I must seek Yahweh's will for myself," he added.

Lappidoth rose and crossed the rooftop. "As any man would do." He rested a hand on Barak's shoulder. "Sleep well, my friend. We will talk again when you are ready."

With a nod toward Deborah, Barak left the rooftop.

"Why is he hesitant?" she whispered to Lappidoth.

He came to her and, with a finger, soothed the creases between her eyes. "Do not worry, my Deborah. This is in Yahweh's hands, not yours."

What could she do but agree? But she spared a fervent prayer that Yahweh would convince the man soon.

CHAPTER SEVENTEEN

The next morning Deborah rose early, as was her custom. She slipped from the bedstead and crept silently from the room, careful not to wake Lappidoth, or Sabra, who had spent a restless night on a mat in the corner of their bedchamber.

While she stood at the worktable, assembling a meal so the family could break their night's fast, Barak emerged from Sabra's bedchamber.

She greeted him quietly. "Was your night restful?"

Taking her cue, he answered in a voice pitched low. "Not especially." His lips twisted into a wry line. "At times Yahweh's direction is as clear to me as a summer's dawn. Other times it is like peering through a fog."

"Last night was fog?" she guessed.

"So thick I could not see my hand if I held it in front of my face." He demonstrated.

"I know the clear dawn as well as the fog." She uncovered a pot of Sabra's cheese, the only one she enjoyed, seasoned with dill and a touch of marjoram.

The line of his lips softened into a near smile. "What? Yahweh leaves even the great prophetess Deborah standing in the fog at times?"

She answered with a question of her own. "Who told you I am a prophetess? I have never laid claim to the title."

"When my brother returned from celebrating Passover at Shiloh, he told me he had heard many people discussing a prophet who had arisen in a small village in the lower part of Ephraim. He discounted the talk as untrue when he heard that the prophet was a woman." He cocked his head sideways. "Until your message arrived."

She felt the weight of his gaze upon her and answered casually while focusing on her hands at work. "I am sure many disregard the talk as heresy, as do some here, in my own village." Asif's outraged face rose up in her mind.

"Not I."

She glanced up at him.

"I learned Yahweh's mitzvah from my imma," he said. "We buried my father when I was not yet ten. Imma made certain her sons honored the covenant of our father Abraham as we grew."

"She taught you Torah?"

"No." His shoulders heaved with a quiet laugh. "She can neither read nor write."

"Not many women can," Deborah said.

"You can."

She shrugged. "Yahweh blessed me with a quick mind and an abba who taught me as he would have taught the son he did not have."

"You are fortunate. Imma may not know much of the holy writings, but she remembers the mitzvah and made sure we followed Yahweh's commands." His eyebrows arched. "Sometimes with force." His eyes became distant, as if focused on a memory.

Deborah had no difficulty imagining Barak as a youth, towering over his imma as she chastised him for breaking a rule.

Her preparations nearly complete, she retrieved a tray from a shelf and began arranging the meal on it. "The others will be up soon, and then we will eat together."

Barak shook his head. "I need to be alone to hear from Yahweh. I feel closest to Him outside, where seeing His creation reminds me of His power."

His words struck her. She, too, felt closest to Yahweh when outside, and alone. She folded bread, figs, and olives inside a square of cloth and tied the ends.

"Here." She handed the bundle to him and then, on impulse, added, "Walk due west a short distance and you will come to a hill. At the top you will find the place where I hear Yahweh's voice most clearly."

His eyes lit. "Deborah's Palm?"

"So I have heard it called," she said. "I prefer to think of it as Yahweh's Palm."

He dipped his head once in acknowledgment and then left the house. She closed her eyes,

I know Your time is not measured as ours is, Yahweh, but I feel an urgency to move forward. Is that from You? If so, speak clearly to him.

Barak did not return to the house, but late morning when Deborah went outside to turn the donkey out to graze, she saw him in the field with Lappidoth, Tivon, and Sabra. Disappointment stabbed at her. Had he prayed, and received his answer? Why did he not come to her and tell her what Yahweh revealed? Recalling Lappidoth's words from the night before, she willed the knots in her stomach to relax. *The matter is not in my hands, but Yahweh's.*

At the sixth hour she climbed the hill to the palm tree and those waiting to hear the day's teaching. Since nearly all the Passover travelers had returned home, most of those gathered on the hillside were known to her—Levi and Anna, Rachel and Shira, Dara, Adena, and Laban, and a dozen others from the village. Uri sat near the front and a little distance from the rest. He wore a frown, and it took Deborah no time at all to realize the reason. Sabra was not there. Apparently she chose to stay in the field today, working alongside her abba and Barak.

Ophira had come also and, to Deborah's surprise, so had her brother Tyrek. Though Deborah had seen Tyrek several times on market days and when he helped with the barley harvest, he had not yet attended her teaching. Nor did he appear happy about being there. He sat with his legs bent, his arms resting upon his knees, and staring sullenly at the ground. Deborah caught Ophira's eye and arched an eyebrow in a question. The young woman glanced at her brother and then rolled her eyes. Deborah resolved to question her later.

She noted a handful of others she did not recognize seated in the back of the group. To those she nodded a greeting.

At the sound of Sabra's voice in the distance, she turned to peer in the direction of their land. To her surprise, she saw her daughter and Barak climbing the hill. Sabra looked like a child next to a giant. She chattered about something, while Barak listened and nodded. Her voice, but not her words, drifted toward Deborah.

When they arrived, Barak gaped at the sight of the small crowd scattered about before the palm tree. He turned a quizzical gaze on Deborah but said nothing. Instead, he followed Sabra to her usual place, in front and to one side. Sabra sat and, to Deborah's surprise, indicated that Barak should sit between her and Uri. The surprise on that arrogant young man's face gave Deborah a moment of satisfaction.

Once everyone settled, Deborah took her accustomed place leaning against the tree and began with the opening blessing. From there she launched into a recitation from *Bereishis,* concerning their father Abraham and the king of Gerar.

As she recounted the story, she felt the weight of Barak's intense stare and was aware that he soaked up every word like rain on dry land. For the first time in many months, she battled nerves. What was he thinking? Would her manner of teaching sway him away from Yahweh's plan or toward it?

But when she ended her recitation and launched into her learnings from the passage, she forgot her worries. Instead, she was swept into the import of the patriarch's actions and Yahweh's healing power in answer to Abraham's prayer.

"Do you see what this account teaches us?" she asked the listeners. "Yahweh honors His covenant. When Abraham was wronged, even though it was through his own foolishness, Yahweh upheld his cause. And we are children of Abraham. Will He not also uphold our cause?" She paused, her gaze sliding from person to person, holding each one for a moment. "I tell you the time is coming when we will see Yahweh's justice. Each one of you within the sound of my voice will see it."

Her voice carried across the hilltop, passion giving her volume. She saw that passion reflected in many of the faces turned toward her. A fervor spread through her, speeding the rhythm of her heartbeat and echoing like a roar in her ears. She closed her eyes, swept up in the breathtaking power that Yahweh would soon unleash in defense of His people. How? She did not know, but that mattered none at all. She trusted Him.

She did not open her eyes until she felt His peace spread throughout her being. When she did, not a soul had moved. An air of anticipation hung in the air. She felt their thoughts press against her. They wanted more.

But she had no more to give.

Raising her hands, she uttered the blessing that closed her teaching. Today the words took on an importance they had not before. For Barak's benefit?

"Be strong, be strong, and let us strengthen each other."

She started to turn away, but a voice stopped her.

"Wait!"

Astonished, she recognized the voice. Uri had never spoken before the others. His verbal jabs and snide remarks were always delivered privately, when no one was close enough to hear. She faced him and was astonished to see no trace of a smirk on his features. In its place was something she could not identify. Bewilderment? Confusion? Or was it fear?

"When?" he asked. "You say we will see Yahweh's justice, but when?"

No one moved. She risked a quick look at Barak. He did not meet her eye but stared at a point on the ground in front of him. Every other gaze fixed on her, waiting. The blood quickened in her veins.

Yahweh, what answer shall I give?

She spoke the first thing that came to mind. "Soon."

"Soon?" Uri leaped to his feet. "What kind of answer is that?"

A sudden calm stole over her. She gave him a serene smile. "The only one I have."

Then she turned toward her home and left them all where they sat.

Barak caught up with her as she arrived at the beehive.

"I was not sure of my answer," he told her. "Not until I heard you speak."

She said nothing. Instead, she checked the lid she had adjusted a few days before to assure herself it remained in place. The anxiety she had battled throughout the morning had fled. On the hilltop, beneath the palm tree, Yahweh had given her a great privilege. He had allowed her to speak with power, His power. Even the small trace she had felt left her trembling in awe. He would see His plan to completion.

"You *are* a prophet. The mouthpiece of Yahweh." His voice filled with awe. "You are the judge He is raising up for this time."

"Israel's judges are warriors." She gave a quiet laugh. "I am no warrior."

"But I am," he said. "Don't you see? You have knowledge. You have wisdom." He paused and waited until she looked up at him. "You hear Yahweh. You are His chosen judge. And I—" Amazement crept over his features, into his voice. "I am your servant."

Deborah shook her head. "We are both His servants."

The buzz from the hives grew loud in the silence that fell between them. She clasped her hands loosely before her, waiting for him to say the words she knew he would say, that he would take up Yahweh's banner and lead His army.

But he did not give the answer she expected.

"I will go," he said. "I will assemble ten thousand men, as Yahweh commands. I will lead them against Sisera's army and, with Yahweh's help, we will emerge victorious. But I will only go if you go with me."

Her mouth fell open. "But I am a woman. Women have no place in wars."

"You are Yahweh's voice, the one to whom he has chosen to reveal His wisdom. Without you, I will fail."

He would not fail. She saw that clearly, and also that she would never convince him.

My King, what shall I do?

Images flitted through her mind. Stars, and swords, and heavy iron chariots pulled by horses. Her ears rang with the sound of metal clashing against metal, of trumpet calls and men's battle cries. Her nose recoiled at the smell of blood.

The sensation faded, leaving her with a thought.

"If you choose this path," she said to Barak, "you will win the day, but the honor of victory will not be yours. If you choose this path, Yahweh will deliver Sisera into the hands of a woman."

He bowed low before her. "I will gladly take no glory for myself but will accord all honor to you."

Deborah opened her mouth to correct him. She would claim no honor, of that she felt certain. But if not she, then who?

It did not matter. If Barak would lead the army, the people would be rid of their Canaanite oppressors. There would be peace in the land. She would leave the details in Yahweh's hands.

But before she agreed, there was one thing she must do.

"I will speak with my husband," she told Barak. "We will decide together."

CHAPTER EIGHTEEN

Deborah found Lappidoth and Tivon in the field, working the barley stubble into the ground. They ceased their work as she approached. Smiling, Lappidoth met her gaze and his smile melted.

"Tivon, go and help your sister herd the goats back to the courtyard."

Tivon's spine stiffened, clearly offended to be dispatched for a menial task. "She needs no help. The goats love her and come at her call."

Lappidoth leveled a stare on their son. "When you are married, you will understand that there are times a husband and wife wish to be alone."

Understanding dawned on his features. With a glance at Deborah, he shouldered his tool and left the field.

When he had passed out of earshot, she said, "I have Barak's answer."

"He will obey Yahweh." There was no hint of doubt in his voice. He searched her face. "But at what cost?"

Steeling herself for his reaction, she said, "He will only go to war with Sisera if I go with him."

Disbelief crept over his features. For a moment he did not speak, and when he did, anger carried his words across the field.

"No!" He shook his head, the movements jerky. "My wife will not go to war. The idea is unthinkable."

Deborah held her tongue as he marched away. She waited, knowing he would return. He gained no more than five lengths' distance before stomping back to her.

"I thought Barak was a man of honor," he barked. "It appears instead he has designs on *my wife!*"

A denial almost burst from her, but with an effort she swallowed it. *Yahweh, speak to him. Impart Your wisdom to him.*

His eyes narrowed. "Did you agree to this foolish scheme?" The question snapped with accusation.

"I did not," she replied calmly. "I told him I would discuss the matter with you and that we would deliver our answer together."

"I will deliver an answer myself." The words ground through gritted teeth. "And he will not like to hear it."

The idea of Lappidoth facing the hulking Barak struck her as humorous. Her lips twitched in her efforts to hold back a laugh.

"I see nothing funny about this…this insane request."

She stepped close to place a hand on his arm. "It is happy laughter, because I see a side of my husband I have never seen. You have never uttered a jealous word in all the years of our marriage."

"It is not jealousy I feel, but fury." In the next moment the hard line of his mouth softened, and he admitted, "Perhaps a small amount of jealousy."

Deborah squeezed his arm. "You well know there is no need."

Searching her face, he finally nodded. "I do." He turned away and raked his fingers through his hair, scrubbing at his scalp. "Nor do I believe Barak has ill intentions toward you. But this request makes no sense. What purpose would a woman serve in battle?"

"A woman?" She shook her head. "None. But a prophetess?" She gulped before speaking the next. "A judge?"

He threw his head back and stared intently at the sky. "When you began the lessons, I told you I would have married you even had I known you would one day become a teacher of Torah. But a judge?"

Pain gripped her heart and sent tears to flood her eyes. "Your answer would be different?"

His chest deflated as he lowered his head to look at her. "How could it be? Yahweh has blessed me with years of contentment. He has filled my home with happiness and my heart with joy. I would not trade one day with you for all the gold in the world." A melancholy smile filled his face. "Am I to say no to Him now, and withhold that blessing from all of Israel?"

The words set the tears free to course down her cheeks, and Deborah threw herself into his arms. He pulled her close and held here there, his breath warm when he whispered in her ear, "But I will not send my wife to war alone. We go together."

They found Barak in the grassy plain beyond their house, helping Tivon and Sabra herd the goats. He saw their approach at a distance and came toward them, taking long strides.

"You have answered Yahweh's call," he said, his eyes gleaming with zeal. "We will go to war together."

"Together." Lappidoth slipped a hand around Deborah's waist. "The three of us."

Grinning up at her husband, she added, "And ten thousand Israelites."

Barak threw his hands high, and his cry of triumph filled the air as Tivon and Sabra came upon them.

"What?" Tivon asked, his gaze sliding between them. "What has happened?"

"Nothing yet." Passion filled Barak's voice. "But soon Jabin and his commander, Sisera, will feel the judgment of Yahweh. Then the whole world will know that He is truly the King of the universe."

"What does that mean?" Sabra came to Lappidoth's side and did not resist when he slid a comforting arm around her. "Will soldiers overrun us?"

"No," Deborah said. "The fighting will take place far to the north of here."

"Where?" Tivon demanded, his voice betraying excitement. "No matter where it is, I will go."

Fear slid inside Deborah's chest and gripped her heart with an iron fist. "You will not, for if you do, you will surely die." The certainty of that prediction nearly took her breath away.

Tivon opened his mouth to protest, but Lappidoth spoke with authority. "Your imma is right. You must stay here and care for the farm and your sister in our absence."

Sabra turned wide eyes on Deborah. "You are going too?"

Tivon whirled on Barak. "You are taking a woman and leaving behind a man fully grown?" He banged a fist against his chest. "What manner of war do you intend to wage?"

The big man folded his arms across his broad chest. "We will wage Yahweh's war."

Before Tivon could respond, Deborah raised her hands to call a halt an argument. "Let us go home, where we can explain." She held Tivon's gaze. "Every decision rests in Yahweh's hands, as you will see."

She walked away, leaving them to follow if they would.

In a way, Tivon's frustration calmed any hesitations Lappidoth had remaining. Deborah and Barak left it to him to describe the steps that had led them to the decision. They sat on the roof in the shade of the canopy. Tivon remained silent, listening to his abba's words with his head bowed.

"So you see," he said at the end of his explanation, "the outcome is not in our hands but in Yahweh's."

Tivon lifted his head. "How do you know it is not Yahweh's plan for me to go with you?"

Deborah answered. "If you go, Adena will be a widow before she is a wife." She held up a hand to forestall an argument. "I know this to be true, and I cannot allow it to happen."

Beside Deborah, Sabra drew in a shuddering breath.

Lappidoth leaned sidewise to nudge his son with an elbow and teased, "It is not always pleasant to have an imma who speaks regularly with Yahweh."

Barak's deep chuckle rumbled in his chest. "Or a wife, I am sure."

Watching her son, Deborah saw the moment he accepted their judgment. His entire body sagged, and her mother's heart ached for him.

"When will you leave?" he asked, despondent.

Deborah looked to Barak for the answer.

"I will leave at dawn," he told them. "When I have assembled ten thousand men, I will send word."

"That will take a long time, will it not?" Sabra's pinched features shouted her worries. "Maybe even a year?"

"Not a year," Barak answered in a soft voice that told her he understood. "But a few months, surely."

"We have time to plan." Lappidoth slapped his hands on his thighs and then got to his feet. "And to make arrangements for our absence. But now, is there any possibility of a meal? My stomach thinks bandits have slit my throat."

Laughing, Deborah rose. She pulled Sabra to her feet to help with the evening meal.

CHAPTER NINETEEN

After Barak left for Naphtali, Deborah's routine returned to normal. She spent her mornings at the house, grinding grain for the day's bread, cleaning the livestock's section of the courtyard, tending vegetables. Evenings were dedicated to seeing to her family's needs.

At midday she climbed the hill and taught Torah to a growing audience. Word of the woman who taught beneath a palm tree spread, and each day brought newcomers from surrounding villages and even other Israelite tribes.

Not only did they come to learn but also to ask for her guidance. She became accustomed to giving advice and even settling disputes.

"My goats wandered into my neighbor's field and ate his vegetables. Now he demands an unreasonable settlement. How much should I offer in recompense?"

"My husband's imma hates me. She dominates our lives, and he defers to her always. What must I do to win his favor?"

"How can I force my brother to give me my share of the inheritance?"

Each time she was presented with a question, Deborah sought Yahweh's wisdom before answering. Often she left the palm tree with a heavy heart, the people's problems pressing on her for days afterward.

"I am barren. I fear my husband will put me away in favor of one who can bear him sons. Will you ask Yahweh to open my womb and make me fruitful?"

A week passed, and then two. Though she knew Barak's task of assembling an army would take time, she found herself looking to the east often, waiting for the messenger who would bid her to come to Naphtali.

One day she climbed the hill, her thoughts focused on the day's teaching. She did not hear footsteps behind her.

"Shalom, Deborah."

Rachel and Shira fell in beside her. She had not seen them for several days.

"I am glad to see you. Are you well? I feared one of you had taken ill."

"We are both well." Rachel scrunched her nose and said, "We sat under Asif's teaching for two days."

Surprised, Deborah looked to Shira. "Asif is teaching Torah?"

The older woman nodded. "Yes, and I am to blame for our absence." Her lips twisted. "I listened to Elinat, who insisted his teaching was good. This morning I told her she has been swayed by comfort and not by good teaching."

Deborah had only a nodding acquaintance with Elinat, who wove baskets and sold them on market days. "Asif's teachings are comfortable?"

"It is not his teachings that are comfortable," Rachel said. "He conducts his meetings in his home."

"He provides cushions." Grinning, Shira patted her backside. "I admit I enjoyed the cushions but not the teacher."

Cushions in his home. Deborah maintained an impartial expression, while inside she seethed. The man's intent was clear. She, a woman, could not invite her listeners into her home lest she risk censure. Her teachings must be conducted in the open, with those who came to hear her seated on the grass.

"Is Asif's home big enough for teaching?" she asked.

"For *his* teaching, yes," Shira said. "The two of us tripled the number, and not a man among us. Perhaps if he were not so dull and tedious, others might come. His house *is* closer to the village." She shook her head. "But he does not have your gift for teaching, Deborah, and he lacks wisdom."

Rachel scowled at her mother. "I feel pity for him. He craves respect, to be thought of as wise."

"My soft-hearted daughter." Shira spared a smile for Rachel. "I find it impossible to pity one so vain. But I do feel for his poor wife, who had to sit through every lesson to ensure he was not alone with a woman."

They walked a few paces in silence while Deborah considered Rachel's soft heart. She was right. Asif's actions were an attempt to overshadow her, to draw attention from her to himself. She had not seen him since the barley harvest, but his words still rang in her ears. *"It is indecent for a woman to teach men."* How it must gall him to have an audience of women, and only a few of them.

"Perhaps his following will grow," she finally said. "If more people seek to learn Torah, then Yahweh is honored."

They reached the crest of the hill. Rachel and Shira joined those assembled to find a place to sit. Gazing over the people before her, Deborah counted more than three dozen, at least half of them strangers from outside the village. A glance showed her there were more men than women.

For a moment she was tempted to gloat, but immediately the lessons from Torah flooded her mind. Yahweh clothed the first man and woman even after they rebelled against him. Mitzvah commanded her to help even her enemy if she found him struggling. To model Yahweh was to show kindness not only to her friends but to everyone.

Forgive me for forgetting. Bestow Your blessing on Asif and his teaching, as You have blessed me beyond measure.

The moment her mind formed the prayer, she felt clean, refreshed. Now she was ready to teach, with nothing in her to taint Yahweh's wisdom. She lifted her hands and spoke the blessing to begin.

"Torah is given to guide us, that we may learn to live in a manner pleasing to Yahweh and in accordance with His mitzvah. And so, we must study the sins of our forefathers, not to repeat them, but to learn from them." She scanned the crowd before her and brought the teaching to an end. She stood and raised her hands to impart the final blessing.

"Teacher, I have a question."

She lowered her hands. Uri had been unusually subdued in recent weeks. Therefore his question, spoken in a voice that carried to those farthest away, surprised her. She was further bewildered when he stood to pose his question. Clasping her hands loosely before her, she waited for him to speak.

"I have heard whisperings involving you, and I want to know if they are true."

Caution stole over her. Was he about to repeat a slur? Accuse her of heresy in front of all those gathered? Coming from him, either was possible, or even worse.

Aware that he had aroused the curiosity of every person present, she asked, "What whisperings have you heard?"

"Is it true that you are amassing an army in the north? That you will attack the Canaanites?"

Deborah's jaw went slack. The air filled with voices whispering to their neighbors, repeating Uri's question. Near the front, Levi and Anna exchanged astonished glances, while Rachel's mouth gaped open, and Shira stared at her through eyes as round as one of Yosef's bowls.

Of all the questions that could be asked of her, this was one Deborah had not anticipated. Uri watched her, his eyes narrowed to slits and his lips twisted into their habitual smirk. Did he hope to put her off guard? To embarrass her, perhaps? It seemed clear that he was not asking out of a desire to know, that he considered whatever whisperings he had heard to be foolish. And what of those whisperings? Where had they come from?

The answer came to her in a flash. Sabra. Anger threatened to rob her of her composure. Had the girl been here, instead of helping Lappidoth in the field, Deborah would have snatched her up, marched her home, and forbidden her to leave the house for years.

She became aware that the voices from the crowd had fallen silent as everyone waited for her to speak.

Yahweh! What shall I say? Has the time come to speak of Your plan? Help me! Use my tongue to speak only what comes from You.

She opened her mouth, not entirely sure what would come out.

"Yes, it is true."

A gasp went up from every throat in the assembly. Now it was Uri's turn to gape in astonishment, a fact that might have given Deborah some satisfaction had she not felt more words bubbling up from her spirit.

She lifted her chin and spoke in a clear, strong voice. "Yahweh showed me a vision in the stars, of the people of Israel united and strong. He whispered to me the name of a man who would wage war with the Canaanites. I sent him a message, and he came." She paced to the left, her gaze sweeping the group. "Some of you met him. Barak from the tribe of Naphtali. He, too, felt Yahweh's call, and has returned to the north to gather an army." She crossed to the right and stopped when she stood in front of Uri. His face had gone pale. "When he is ready, he will send for me. Together we will go to war."

A man from the back jumped to his feet. "Do you know what this means?" He ran to the front, to Deborah's side. "Yahweh has returned to us." Tears streamed down his face and disappeared into his beard. "He has bestowed His favor on us once more."

Others leaped up, hands and voices raised. They shouted praises toward the heavens. Shira grabbed Rachel and swung her around in an exuberant dance, and others joined in.

The man beside her, with tears still falling freely, gazed at Deborah in awe. "You are the one. The judge Yahweh has chosen to lead us." To her astonishment, he fell to his knees at her feet. "When you go, I will go with you. I will fight Yahweh's battle at your side."

"As will I," shouted someone, and a chorus of others joined in.

A fierce exultation consumed Deborah's being. She lifted her face to the sky, and a song burst unbidden from her mouth.

"My joy is in Yahweh, and I will sing His praise.
He is my strength and my song.
I will trust, and not be afraid
For He will deliver His children.
He will crush their enemies
And restore His peace in the land."

When she fell silent, others took up her song and repeated it. There, on the hilltop before the palm tree, the people celebrated and worshiped Yahweh. Watching them, feeling their devotion and reverence, Deborah knew she was glimpsing the jubilation that would spread throughout Israel when her vision was fulfilled. She surged forward and grasped hands with Anna and Rachel and gave herself over to worshiping Yahweh in dance.

Only later did she realize Uri had left the hill.

CHAPTER TWENTY

"May I come with you to visit Adena?" Standing behind the worktable, Deborah looked up to see Tivon's reaction to his sister's request. Creases erupted on his brow, and he opened his mouth to voice what would surely be a refusal. With a hand motion, Deborah caught his attention and frowned. Her meaning was clear.

Tivon heaved a resigned sigh. "You may come," he told Sabra, "but if you cheat at *senet,* I will drag you home by the hair."

She drew herself up. "I do not cheat. You are jealous because I am a better player than you."

Watching them leave the house, still arguing, Deborah shook her head in amusement.

A month had passed since the announcement on the hilltop, and still no message from Barak. Though logic told her the gathering of ten thousand fighting men would take time, she grew impatient. Every day saw new visitors to the palm tree, full of questions. They demanded to hear about her vision in the stars, which she repeated almost daily. Though the spontaneous spirit of worship that overcame that momentous day did not occur again, the people rejoiced at the news that Yahweh had heard the cries of His people and would soon act on their behalf.

How soon? The question was posed over and over, and her answer did not change. *In Yahweh's time.*

She finished clearing the worktable and, taking a jug of milk from the storeroom, climbed the stairs to join Lappidoth on the roof. She found him wielding the heavy roller they kept there, compacting an area of loosened clay. Seeing her, a smile broke out on his face and he rolled the tool to the corner, where they stored it.

"Just the thing," he said, taking a cup and watching as she poured fresh milk into it. "My sleep has been uneasy lately. Maybe this will help."

She knew he had not rested peacefully recently. He tossed about on the bedstead until the early morning hours, disturbing Deborah with each movement.

After filling her own cup, she followed him to the mats still laid out from their evening meal. They sat leaning against the surrounding wall, close enough to touch each other.

"What worries interrupt your sleep?" she asked.

He responded instantly. "Sabra."

She should have guessed. Concern for their daughter plagued her as well.

"No response from your brothers and cousins?"

He peered at her in surprise, and then his expression cleared. "It is not thoughts of her betrothal that worry me. But no, no response."

Curious, she asked, "If not the betrothal, then what?"

He shifted his position so that he sat facing her. "What will become of her when we join Barak in the north? She cannot stay here with Tivon, no matter what we told him."

He spoke the truth. Tivon was a trustworthy young man, and he cared for his sister even though they quarreled frequently. But he was not a parent. He could not supervise her all day, especially when he was tasked with taking care of their farm.

"I worry that she will be here, in this house, unprotected." His eyes darkened. "What if Uri son of Gersham hears that she is alone?"

"Uri has not come to my teachings since he forced me into announcing Yahweh's plans for war," she told him.

The young man's absence had both relieved and disturbed her. Though she far preferred teaching without being constantly confronted by his arrogant stares, her thoughts drifted to him often. Why had he given up on plaguing her? Had he finally accepted her decision that he would never have Sabra as his wife? Or had the knowledge of the upcoming battle frightened him so deeply that he was determined to distance himself from any discussion on the subject? Whatever his reason, perhaps his absence was Yahweh's doing.

"He may be maintaining his distance from you," Lappidoth said, "but you will not be here."

Deborah sipped from her cup, her thoughts busy. "She could stay with Dara and Chaim. I am sure they would welcome her."

"I thought of them as well," he said. "We could send her to my brother in Gezer."

"Or take her to my sister in Shiloh on our way to Naphtali," she added.

They fell into a contemplative silence. Deborah reviewed each possibility but felt no peace in her spirit for any.

Lappidoth turned again to lean against the wall. "We must wait on Yahweh. He will provide an answer."

She bit back a comment that lately she seemed to wait on Yahweh's answers more often than not. Shame filled her at the thought.

Forgive me, Yahweh. You asked me to trust You, and I do.

If only His answers came more quickly.

When Deborah reached the top of the hilltop the next day, she stopped in surprise. She had grown accustomed to larger numbers, but today's assembly was different. Tents lined three sides of the area where her listeners gathered, and a small herd of donkeys grazed behind them. Men sat before some of the tents, while others worked to erect another at the back of the assembly. The villagers she knew. Ophira and her sullen brother Tyrek, who no doubt had been forced to come by his sister. Besides them, Rachel and Shira, Levi and Anna, Dara and Adena. All sat watching with bemused expressions.

Someone noticed her arrival. A male voice shouted, "She has arrived."

Those working on the tent stopped, as did all conversations. Deborah's gesture swept the tents. "What is this?"

A man seated in the closest tent rose. "I am Eliakim, of the tribe of Benjamin," he said as he paced toward her. "We have heard of the judge who sits beneath Deborah's Palm, and of her holy war against the Canaanites." He pounded a fist on his chest. "We have come to fight for Israel."

"I am Deborah." She laid a hand on the thick tree trunk. "And as you can see, I teach beneath a palm tree. But the coming war is not mine. It is Yahweh's."

Eliakim's eyes gleamed. "And with Yahweh's help, we will win the day."

A roar went up from the company, a deafening shout of victory that rose into the sky.

Did they come in belief that the army would march from here, from this tiny village in Ephraim? Deborah exchanged a glance with Dara, whose eyes were so wide they appeared in danger of falling out of her head. She gave a very slight shake of her head and shrugged one shoulder.

Her mouth dry, Deborah raised her hands for silence. "Yahweh has called a man, Barak of the tribe of Naphtali, to assemble and lead Israel's army. Even now he is in the north, gathering men to march against the Canaanite commander Sisera."

"Then the end of our journey lies in Naphtali," Eliakim said. "But first we will camp a few days here, so we may learn from Yahweh's chosen judge and prophet."

He bowed low at the waist before returning to his tent.

Deborah tried to clear her jumbled thoughts. The sight of the men, and their passion to fight for Israel, left her so numb for a moment she could not remember the day's lesson. When she did, she nearly laughed with delight. The Torah section she had chosen came from BaMidbar, the fourth book, when Yahweh waged war against the Midianites.

She clapped to draw everyone's attention. "Today we will hear of another time when Yahweh sent the nation of Israel to war, and we will see the justice of the King of the universe against those who oppress His people."

During her recitation of the passage, her listeners gave her their full attention. Not a sound was heard to interfere with her voice. When she launched into the teaching, the men from Benjamin bent toward her, absorbing her words like a thirsty man gulps water.

"What can we learn from this act of Yahweh's vengeance?" Her gaze swept the crowd. "That Yahweh's memory is long, stretching far into the past, and that He does not forget a single wrong done to the children of Israel. He stirs men to act." She smiled toward the Benjamites. "As He is doing now."

"What is this foolish women's prattle?"

The voice came from behind the palm tree and carried far. She turned in time to see Asif stride toward her. In recent weeks she had been spared from encounters with him, though she heard he had given up holding Torah lessons in his house when his students dwindled to two.

When he saw the crowd, and the tents, his step faltered. But only for the briefest of moments. His expression hardened and he came to a stop beside her.

"What do you mean by this?" he demanded of her. "You are full of deceit, and your mouth full of lies."

An angry rumble rolled through the watchers. Deborah held up a hand to quiet them, though kept her eyes fixed on Asif.

"To what lies are you referring?" Her voice betrayed no hint of the knots that tangled her insides. "Do you dispute the truth of Torah?"

"By no means." He leaned closer. "I dispute your flawed teaching that you present as based on Torah. I am surprised Yahweh has not struck you down where you stand."

"Please correct my *flawed teaching*." She gestured toward the crowd. "Tell us. What would Yahweh have us learn from the destruction of the Midianites?"

His mouth flapped open as he looked out over the people.

When he made no answer, she said, "The battle, and Yahweh's instructions, are described in BaMbidar. It follows His instructions concerning the relationship between a man and his wife."

"I know where the passage is," he snapped. "I have taught on that very battle myself."

She folded her arms across her chest and waited.

"I will not speak here." His hand waved in the air, toward the palm fronds that waved in a breeze above their heads. "This place is ill suited for holy teachings."

And your house was better?

Whether Yahweh stilled her tongue or she did it herself she did not know, but she was glad. There was no gain to be had in trading insult for insult.

A commotion sounded from one side. She turned to find three of the Benjamites striding toward them.

"Who is this, and why does he interrupt your teaching?"

The tallest of the three, who stood nearly the height of Barak, advanced until Asif had to crane his neck to look the man in the face.

"Who are you?" Asif fired back.

"I am Oded." The man growled his answer. "I am a soldier in Yahweh's army. And you have interrupted Yahweh's chosen judge."

Asif turned an incredulous stare on her. "It is true. You *are* amassing an army under the guise of being guided by Yahweh. I thought it to be the gossiping of demented people." He took a backward step, away from the hulking man before him, and addressed the watchers. "You are being deceived. Why would Yahweh entrust His plans to a woman?"

The three from Benjamin advanced on him, closing him in between them.

"Friend," said Eliakim, "I think it is time for you to leave."

"I am not your friend," Asif spat, and then stabbed a finger in Deborah's direction. "And neither is she." He whirled to make his exit but stopped before he began the descent. Fixing a glare on her, he said, "Since you know Torah so well, you would benefit from heeding the lesson Yahweh gave concerning husbands and wives. I am sure you know the one."

He marched down the hill and was soon lost from sight.

Though trouble stirred in her spirit, she smiled at the three who had come to her aid. "Thank you."

Oded said, "Take nothing he said to heart. Small men often shout the loudest."

As the men returned to their tent, Dara came forward and wrapped Deborah in a comforting embrace. Though she had stood firm to Asif's face, now that he was gone her knees trembled. She clung to Dara for a long moment, drawing strength from her friend.

"What did Asif mean about husbands and wives?" Dara whispered.

"The section from Torah concerns a wife who makes a vow or pledges herself under oath." Her throat felt dry, even swollen, stung by the barb of his parting comment. "Yahweh told Moses if the husband accepts her pledge, then he must suffer the consequences of her wrongdoing."

When Deborah came down the hill in the company of Dara, Ophira, and the others, Lappidoth met them beneath the fig trees. Deborah searched his face as they drew near, and noted the deep creases between his eyebrows, a sure sign of distress. She did not need to guess at the cause. Lappidoth had been working in the field all afternoon, which meant Asif would have passed by on his way to and from the village.

Before she could say anything, Shira spoke.

"You should have been at the palm tree," the elderly woman told Lappidoth. "Quite a stir up there today."

He responded with a tight smile. "So I have been told."

"To think I would live to see armed men sit under the teaching of a woman. And leap to her defense." She rubbed her hands together and cackled with delight. "What a day."

Deborah would have joined in her laughter had Lappidoth not worn such a sober expression.

"Thank you for coming today," Deborah told her companions. "At times I feel as if the world is moving so quickly my head spins, and all I have to hold on to are the hands of my friends."

They bid her goodbye and continued on their way, leaving her alone with Lappidoth.

"Will you walk with me?" he asked.

When she nodded, they fell in beside each other, wandering through the orchard of fig trees. Pink flowers crowded the branches above their heads, signs of a good harvest in the fall. A thought struck her.

"I hope we are here to see the figs ripen."

How long did wars take? Some went on for years, while others were decided in a single battle. She prayed this one would be short.

Lappidoth remained silent, walking with his head down and his hands clasped behind his back.

"Something disturbs you," she said. "Is it Asif?"

His lips twisted into a wry line, and he nodded. "He approached me in the field to discuss a matter. While we talked, we heard a shout from the hilltop, a roar from the throats of many men."

"Benjamites," she told him. "They have heard of the coming war and came to join the battle." She hesitated. "They are still here, but plan to continue north in a few days."

He showed no surprise, or any reaction at all, further proof that his thoughts distracted him.

"Asif came with an offer." He did not look at her but continued his slow, measured pace. "An offer of betrothal for Sabra."

"What?" she asked, stunned. Asif's sons were grown and married long ago. "With whom?"

"A nephew, the son of a sister who lives in a remote region in Ephraim's northwest, near the Manasseh border. She wrote to Asif with an inquiry, since there are few prospects in their small community. He is fifteen."

Young for a bridegroom but better than a widower with three children. Sabra would stay at home until the boy was old enough to provide for a wife. That they might have several more years with their daughter pleased her, and no doubt Lappidoth as well. And a betrothal would shut Uri out of their lives. Still, an offer from Asif to join his family with theirs? It was so out of character it was unbelievable.

"How did you answer him?" she asked.

"I could find no fault with the idea. The mohar Asif mentioned was acceptable. He asked if I would meet with the boy and his abba if they traveled here." He glanced sideways at her. "I agreed."

Her thoughts flew to their journey to Naphtali, and the coming conflict. "They must make haste, or they will find us gone."

"I thought the same and said as much. That is when we heard the shout. Asif left me standing in the field."

He did not need to tell her where Asif went. "He came to the palm tree," she said quietly. "We had a…" She searched for a word. "A disagreement."

The wry smile returned. "I guessed as much from his manner when he returned."

Picturing the man's fury as he marched away, Deborah could imagine the scene when he returned to Lappidoth. "He withdrew his offer."

"Not at all. But he set a condition in place." Lappidoth stopped and faced her. "You must give up what he termed *'this charade, passing herself off as the savior of Israel.'* Only then will he sanction the betrothal."

Emotions battled inside her, and her hands clenched into fists. Anger that the man would make such a demand of her. Indignation at the suggestion that she reject Yahweh's plan for her, and for all of Israel. Scorn for his arrogance in attempting to displace her as teacher. But beneath those, an overwhelming grief that ached deep in her soul. This divine assignment that had become her passion was hurting her family. Most painful of all was the sorrow she saw on her husband's face.

She became aware that Lappidoth was watching her closely, waiting for her response.

"What would you have me do?" she asked him. "Send word to Barak and tell him I have changed my mind? Deny the vision Yahweh gave me?" She waved a hand in the direction of her palm tree. "Give up teaching?"

When he did not answer at first, alarm stretched her muscles tight. Would he ask that of her?

Finally, his chest deflated with a sigh, and he shook his head. "No. You are Yahweh's chosen instrument. Even if I could deny you, how could I deny Him?"

He opened his arms, and she stepped into his embrace. Standing there, with his arms around her, she whispered a prayer of thanksgiving.

"But I do long for the days when you were merely my wife and not Israel's prophetess and judge," he said, his breath warm against her ear.

An ache throbbed in her chest. "I know."

He pulled back. "If we are not home soon, Tivon will recruit your Benjamites to search for us."

"They are not *my* Benjamites," she told him primly.

Arm in arm, they turned toward their home.

When Lappidoth put his hand to the courtyard gate, Sabra appeared in the doorway.

"We have a visitor," she announced.

They were expecting no one. Before Deborah could ask, a woman appeared at Sabra's side.

She planted her hands on her hips and demanded, "What is this I hear about my niece teaching Torah like a prophet and marching off to war?"

"*Doda* Yocheved?" Deborah peered at the woman, hardly daring to believe her eyes.

A grin broke out on the woman's face. She threw her arms wide and ran toward them. In the next moment,

Deborah found herself nearly smothered against an ample bosom.

"What are you doing here?" she asked when she was released.

"Is that any way to greet your abba's favorite sister?" She slid an arm through Deborah's and Lappidoth's and pulled them toward the house. "Come inside. Have a cup of wine while your delightful daughter and I finish the meal."

"Has my *dohd* come as well?" Deborah remembered her uncle as a cheerful man, always laughing. The perfect husband for the jovial Yocheved.

Yocheved's face fell, her jolly mood gone in an instant. "My husband rests with his ancestors."

Deborah bowed her head, sorrow squeezing her heart.

"I miss him," Yocheved said, and then dimples appeared in her plump cheeks. "But he always said he looked forward to getting to know his ancestors when the time came. No doubt he is keeping them entertained with a lifetime of jokes. And better them than me, for I heard them all a dozen times over."

What could Deborah do but laugh?

Yocheved dropped their arms and scurried around the worktable, where Sabra was pouring honey into a bowl of dried dates from last year's harvest. She watched the older woman with a bemused expression.

Yocheved picked up a knife and began slicing a cucumber with rapid gestures that Deborah feared might result in the loss of a finger.

"So when news reached me about a woman prophet named Deborah who was bent on stirring up trouble in the north, I said to myself, 'Yocheved, get yourself down there and find out what kind of mischief your niece is into.'" She adopted a nasally voice and swung the knife in the air like a sword as she talked. Sabra giggled, and Yocheved grinned at her. "And being a poor, helpless widow with nothing to stop me, I decided to listen to myself, and here I am."

Deborah knew Yocheved was anything but helpless, or poor. Her husband had owned a vineyard, and his grapes were prized all across Ephraim. Since Yahweh had not blessed the pair with children, she suspected he had left his wife lacking nothing.

"We are glad to have you," she told Yocheved.

Lappidoth wore a dazed expression, as if not sure what to make of this boisterous relative who had invaded their home.

Yocheved lifted an eyebrow in his direction. "She says that now, but I know full well people can only take so much of me. When it is time for me to go, you say the word. I will pack my belongings and be gone in a wink." She paused and then corrected herself. "As soon as a cart comes from the village to help, that is. I brought more than I can carry myself."

Sabra nodded her agreement. "You should see my bedchamber. There are crates and bundles everywhere."

Deborah watched her husband, waiting for him to speak.

"We are blessed to have you," he said finally. "You are welcome here for as long as you wish to stay."

Deborah relaxed and poured gratitude into the smile she gave him.

"Did you hear that?" Yocheved asked Sabra. "Me, a blessing." She lowered her voice and said in a loud whisper meant to be overheard. "We will see if he thinks the same after a few days."

Again, Sabra giggled, and Deborah rejoiced to see her daughter in such high spirits.

Lappidoth caught her eye and dipped his head in the direction of their bedchamber. She followed him.

"Your prayers have been answered. Yahweh sent her here." He glanced toward the common room, where Doda Yocheved could be heard regaling Sabra with a tale from her youth. "We can leave Sabra and Tivon in her care when we go to Naphtali."

The ache returned to her heart at the sight of his slumped back and downcast expression.

Deborah wrapped her arms around him and pulled him close. "He has yet to answer my most ardent prayer. That my husband would be as committed to His plan as I am, and be filled with peace."

"I am committed," he said.

She waited for him to continue, but he did not. Closing her eyes, she formed a silent prayer. *Yahweh, give him peace.*

CHAPTER TWENTY-ONE

The next day saw a merry troop climbing the hill. Not only their friends and neighbors, but Lappidoth and Tivon came in early from their work in the field so they could meet the Benjamites who camped there. Deborah and Sabra exchanged amused glances as Yocheved kept up a constant stream of chatter, which rendered even the outspoken Shira speechless.

"And then my husband said to the wool merchant"—she adopted a deep voice—"'What a blessing you have been able to produce such fine *wool* even in the midst of a dangerous *woolf*.'"

Peals of laughter overtook her, and she had to stop her climb to catch her breath.

Walking beside Deborah, Lappidoth groaned.

"What a jokester your husband was," Tivon said, battling a grin. "I regret not knowing him."

"Ah, you would have loved him," she said. "Everyone did."

They crested the hill then, and Yocheved stopped, her gaze sweeping the area and her jaw dangling open. She turned to Deborah, her eyes wide.

"I confess I thought the rumors of your following were mostly gossip, but I was wrong." She looked again at the gathering. "The talk does not give you enough credit."

Heat crept into Deborah's cheeks. "The credit belongs to Yahweh. These are His followers, not mine."

"But you are Yahweh's mouthpiece," Levi said, and several others nodded their agreement.

Yocheved marched to the palm tree and laid a hand on the trunk, gazing upward into the leafy growth far above. "Deborah's Palm." Her bosom swelled as she drew a deep, satisfied breath. "To think I would live to see the day."

Catching sight of Deborah, the southerners came forward as a group, greetings on their lips. She stood back, watching as the two groups made themselves known to each other. Even those seated on the grass, most of whom were known to her, but a few who were not, rose to join in the welcoming chatter.

Finally, Deborah clapped her hands and, with a laugh in her voice, announced, "If we do not start soon, the sun will set before I finish the day's teaching."

"So much the better," said the tallest Benjamite.

They all took their seats, Yocheved in the center of the first row.

Deborah raised her hands and spoke the opening blessing.

Throughout the teaching, Yocheved held her tongue, though several times she nodded with such vigor that Deborah expected her to leap to her feet and express her agreement. Even afterward, when a line formed of people waiting to ask Deborah's judgment on their personal situations, she remained respectfully quiet.

Not until Deborah spoke a blessing over the last person did the robust woman call for attention.

"Many of you have come from far away to hear our Deborah teach. I look around and see people who are hungry for Yahweh's wisdom, and I wonder." She tapped her lips with a finger as though considering a great mystery. "What else might you be hungry for?"

Quiet laughter at her turn of phrase rumbled from the watchers.

"Therefore, I would like to invite you all to a feast," she said. "Tomorrow at sundown, come to the home of Lappidoth, and together we will celebrate the upcoming victory that Yahweh will deliver into your hands."

Deborah cast a quick glance at Lappidoth, whose skin had gone pasty and eyes bulged with panic. She hurried forward and plucked at her aunt's robe.

"Feeding all these people will empty our storeroom," she said in a low voice. "We will have nothing left to feed ourselves."

Yocheved planted her hands on her hips. "Did you not just speak of Yahweh's provision when our people wandered in the desert?"

Those in their immediate vicinity watched, waiting for Deborah's answer.

"Yes, but—"

One of the travelers spoke up. "We carried food for our journey, enough to share."

"We were blessed with a bountiful harvest." Dara looked to Chaim, who nodded. "I will make bread for the meal."

"You see?" Yocheved said. "If there is one thing I have learned over the course of my many years, it is that Yahweh enjoys a good celebration."

Deborah watched Lappidoth, who wore the same bemused expression that had appeared often since Yocheved's arrival. He caught Deborah's eye and shrugged.

"Then let us gather and celebrate Yahweh together," she said, and was answered by a cheer.

As the Benjamites returned to their tents and those who lived nearby left for their homes, Yocheved called Tivon to her side. From somewhere in her voluminous robes, she withdrew a heavy pouch. The clink of many coins sounded as she reached inside. These she pressed into Tivon's hand.

"Go to the village or the fields and purchase meat for our feast. A cow and a few plump sheep. And if you know a good cook, I am partial to apricot sweet cakes."

Looking at the coins, Tivon's eyes widened, and he nodded.

"Sabra!" She looked around until she located Sabra talking with Adena. She looked up when her name was called. "Come, girl. We have work to do."

Deborah watched as, arm in arm, they marched down the hill.

⚬━━⚬━━⚬

The following evening the grassy area around Deborah's house filled with merrymakers. Yocheved had spent the day overseeing the roasting of the meat, and the aroma wafted through the air all the way up the hill to the palm tree. Her listeners fidgeted during the teaching, and she ended the lesson earlier than usual. Not a single person lined up to ask for her judgment or even spared more than a "Thank you" as they hurried down the hill toward the feast.

And feast it was. In that area, where most people lived by modest means, meat was considered an occasional treat and saved for special occasions. Somehow word spread through the village, and Deborah spied several people who had never attended one of her teachings. Not a woman arrived without a food offering of her own. Lentils stewed with onions, melons, carobs, grapes, figs, cucumbers, leeks, cheese—more food than even that huge crowd could easily consume.

Shira arrived with a platter piled high with oat cakes sweetened with apricots and presented them proudly to Yocheved, who snatched one and bit into it.

"The best I have ever tasted," she proclaimed. "A delicacy fit for royalty."

Preening, Shira carried the rest to the place where Deborah and Dara had spread rugs to hold the food.

The southerners arrived carrying their travel rations, which Yocheved refused to take.

"You will need those for your journey," she told them. "And for the war. No one knows how long it might go on."

People stood in small groups or seated themselves on the grass to talk with one another, while children chased each other between them, their high-pitched laughter rising above the adults' voices. Women gathered around Ophira, whose pregnancy was now apparent to casual observers, exchanging tales from the births of their own children. One of the men from Benjamin arrived with a lute and soon had his own gathering as he strummed and led them in a song of praise in a low, melodic voice.

Deborah stood a little apart, listening to his words of praise. Everywhere she looked, happy people smiled and laughed. For a moment she glimpsed what Moses might have seen as he listened to the people praise Yahweh in song for giving them water in the desert.

Except Mosha would have joined in the song instead of standing idly by, listening.

Amused by her own wry thought, Deborah started toward the singers. Then her gaze snagged on Sabra at the far corner of the courtyard, talking to Uri son of Gersham. They had not seen him in many weeks, and she had hoped—prayed—that he had given up his idea of a relationship with her daughter. Muscles instantly taut, she changed direction and started toward them.

Yocheved chose that moment to raise her voice above the noise of the crowd.

"What a fine gathering we have," she shouted. Voices hushed as people turned their attention to her. "And what a feast. Welcome to all. Before we begin, our host will bless the abundance of food Yahweh has provided through your hands."

Lappidoth raised his hands and lifted his face toward the heavens.

"Blessed are You, Yahweh, King of the universe, who brings forth bread from the earth, and fruit from the vine, and who creates varieties of nourishment. Blessed are You, Yahweh, knower of secrets, who calls us to holiness through mitzvah, commanding us to pursue justice. Blessed are You, Yahweh, at whose word all came to be."

A moment of reverent silence rested over the crowd when his voice ceased.

And then Yocheved shouted. "Let us fill our bellies with Yahweh's bounty."

In the next instant, Deborah stepped aside to avoid being trampled as people rushed for the food. When she looked again, she found Sabra assisting Yocheved in slicing the meat. Uri had joined a line of young men waiting their turn at the food-covered rugs. Determined to keep an eye on the pair, she went to join Sabra at the roasting pit.

"We have a latecomer," Sabra said when Deborah approached.

She pointed in the distance, and Deborah looked in that direction. A lone figure approached from the north.

Yocheved finished cutting a serving of mutton and looked as well. "I will not turn anyone away. Though if he tarries much longer the apricot cakes will be gone."

Deborah narrowed her eyes, straining to identify the man. "I do not recognize him."

"Probably someone who has heard of the woman prophet and comes to hear your teaching," Sabra said.

"Go and greet him, Deborah. Tell him he is welcome." Yocheved returned to her task.

Deborah left the heat of the roasting pit. When Lappidoth saw her, he left the men with whom he was talking and joined her.

"Shalom," Lappidoth said when they were close enough to exchange greetings.

"Shalom," the man responded. "I come with a message for Deborah, who has been named judge and prophetess of Israel."

Startled by his words, she glanced at her husband before saying, "I am Deborah."

He unslung a leather pouch at his side and withdrew a tablet. "I am to place this in your hands, and none other."

As he handed the tablet to her, his gaze strayed over her shoulder.

Lappidoth noticed. "We have just begun to eat," he said. "Please join us and be welcome."

The messenger's eyes lit. Mumbling his thanks, he hurried in that direction.

Deborah untied a strip of cloth and lifted the piece of wood that served to protect the message pressed into the clay tablet. As she read the brief notation, an unearthly numbness crept over her. She looked up into Lappidoth's face and found that she could not speak. Wordlessly, she handed the tablet to him.

He read the missive aloud. "'Barak son of Abinoam, sends greetings to Deborah and Lappidoth in Ephraim. The army is assembled. Come with all speed to Hamath in Naphtali, beside the Sea of Galilee.'" He lifted his face and his gaze locked on to hers. Reluctance lurked in the depths of his eyes. "It has begun."

She managed a whisper through her tight throat. "Yahweh, help us."

CHAPTER TWENTY-TWO

"And if we are not back by the time you harvest the figs, please feed one to the she-goats every few days," Deborah instructed Sabra. "They love them."

"I know, Imma. I was here for last fall's harvest, remember?" Though Sabra responded in a respectful tone, Deborah sensed she was frustrated by a long string of instructions.

They stood in front of the courtyard gate surrounded by a troop of men and donkeys, all laden with supplies for the journey to Hamath. Two days had passed since Barak's message arrived. Deborah and Lappidoth would travel north in the company of the Benjamites, an arrangement that relieved her mind of worries that she had not voiced aloud. A couple on the road presented an easy target for bandits, but an entire troop of men carrying weapons on their backs? Thieves would go to lengths to avoid them.

Deborah rubbed the donkey's velvety nose. "I am sorry you will miss your favorite treat," she told the animal. The animal carried a load of bundles containing her and Lappidoth's supplies strapped to its back.

"Listen to you," Yocheved scolded. "The figs will not ripen for four months yet. You will return long before then."

"I hope you are right."

The big woman planted her hands on her hips. "Can you name a time when I was wrong?"

Laughing, Deborah pulled her into an embrace. "I cannot think of a single instance." She whispered in her ear. "Remember what I said, please."

Deborah had given explicit instructions that Yocheved should keep Sabra away from Uri as much as possible, and when she could not, to stay right beside them.

"Leave the matter in my hands," Yocheved whispered back. "When I finish with that boy, he will be afraid to even look in her direction."

Deborah had no doubt she would make good on her promise.

Next she moved to Sabra. "I shall pray every day that Yahweh will keep you safe."

"And I will do the same for you." Sabra threw her arms around Deborah and hugged her tightly. "I will miss you, Imma. Please do not put yourself in danger. Promise me that you will stay away from the fighting."

Tears prickled at the back of Deborah's eyes. She could not make that promise with any certainty of keeping it. She placed a tender kiss on her daughter's head. "I will be guided by Yahweh's hand."

Tivon stood at the donkey's head, holding the rope. Taking his face in her hands, she pulled him close and kissed his brow.

A smile twitched at the corners of his lips. "What? Have you no advice? No reminders for me?"

"You are a man fully grown," she replied. "You need no reminders from your imma." Then she grinned. "And I know your abba has listed them all in great detail."

"Imma, look."

Sabra pointed to the east, where two figures and a donkey had just crested a rise in the land

"It is Uri," Sabra said.

"And Gersham." Lappidoth stepped up to Deborah's side, his voice heavy with disbelief. "They are dressed for travel."

Each wore a travel robe and carried a walking stick. When they drew near, Sabra ran to meet them. Deborah was so stunned by their appearance she could not muster an objection.

"I see we are in time," Uri said by way of greeting.

"In time to see us off?" Deborah asked, still not comprehending what her eyes told her.

"In time to travel with you." His usual smirk appeared. "We are going to war."

Deborah looked from him to Gersham, who stood scowling beneath unruly eyebrows.

"I am good with a sword," he growled.

Try though she might, Deborah could think of no reply. What purpose had Yahweh in this? Their presence must be a part of His plan. He must have nudged these idolaters to join them. Nothing less than divine direction could explain their presence.

Eliakim strode forward to join them. "Shalom and be welcome. Two more soldiers for Yahweh's army."

Had she not been staring at Gersham, she would have missed the curl of his lip. In an instant it was gone, but its appearance confirmed for her what she guessed. Gersham had not experienced a change of heart about Yahweh. He wanted to join them only to keep his son safe.

And Uri? She slid her gaze to the son. What purpose did he have in joining Yahweh's holy war?

Trust.

Yahweh's answer to her worries about Uri once again resounded in her soul.

Yocheved sidled up to Deborah and whispered, "That is one less thing for me to worry about."

Deborah nodded. There was that, anyway. She would not be plagued by worries about Uri's attention to Sabra while she was gone.

"Let us be off, then." Eliakim peered at Lappidoth. "Unless you know of others who plan to join us?"

In answer, he splayed his hands. "I did not know of these two. But no, I do not think there will be others."

"One more will join us." Uri's expression became smug as he looked at Deborah. "Tyrek will join us when we pass through the village."

She could not stop her jaw from dangling. Tyrek, Ophira's wayward brother who walked about with a sullen frown and glutted himself of on stolen wine?

"Why?" she finally managed.

Uri shrugged. "Perhaps he merely wants to kill Canaanites."

Eliakim threw his head back and his booming laugh carried to the sky. "Whoever this Tyrek is, we will take ten thousand like him."

He picked up a heavy bundle, slung it across his back, and struck out northward. The others fell in behind him. Lappidoth took the donkey's rope from Tivon and turned to her.

With a last look at her home and her children, Deborah strode to his side, and together they joined the others.

They pushed hard the first day and crossed the border to Manasseh just before sunset. Making camp in a desolate region, they unloaded the beasts and set them to graze. Eliakim sent a handful of men to search for firewood and another to scout the area to make sure there were no thieves lurking nearby.

Deborah stood to one side while Lappidoth and Tyrek removed their bundles and sent the donkey to forage with the others. Ophira's sullen brother had joined them in the village, carrying a heavy load on his back. Seeing him, she had worried that he did not have the strength or the stamina of the southern men and would soon struggle to keep up. Lappidoth must have thought the same, for he offered to add the young man's burden to theirs.

When their belongings had been piled on the ground, Deborah collapsed and leaned against them. Never had she felt so tired, her limbs so heavy.

Lappidoth rummaged in a pack and handed her a skin of water. "Are your feet as sore as mine?"

She could not muster the strength to answer. Instead, she nodded as she unstrapped her sandals and tossed them away with force. Laughing, he dropped to the ground beside her.

"I will build a fire like the others if you want," he said, "but I see no need. A piece of dried mutton and a bite of bread before I fall asleep will suffice for me. Unless you want the comfort of a fire?"

"I am not sure I have the strength to chew." Her eyelids drifted shut before she finished speaking.

"Some warriors we are." He chuckled. "But at least we are not the only ones."

She opened her eyes and followed his gaze. Tyrek lay on the grass nearby with one arm thrown across his eyes. A soft snore rose from his open mouth.

"Days spent at the potter's wheel build strength in different muscles than laboring in the field," she said. Then she laughed at herself. In another few minutes she, too, would be asleep on the ground. "While teaching beneath a palm tree builds none at all."

Someone approached from behind, and she glanced up to see Uri. Even he looked tired, though at least he was still on his feet.

"Where is your abba?" Lappidoth asked.

"Gone to find Eliakim. He wants to ask about the rest of the journey and when we might reach Hamath."

"I wonder the same." Lappidoth stood, looked in the distance, and then strode away.

Uri remained to stare down at her.

"You were surprised when we joined you this morning," he said.

"I was," she agreed. "You have not come to the palm tree since the day after Barak left, when you forced me to speak of the coming war. I thought you had no interest in Yahweh or His plans."

"Perhaps you are right." He paused and then went on in a softer voice. "Or perhaps there is a different reason."

"What reason would that be?"

"You know my family does not practice the old religion, as you do." He lifted his shoulders in a shrug. "Perhaps I was dissuaded from returning by my brothers. And my abba."

Exhaustion muddled her mind and rendered her too tired to guard her tongue. "Are you not of age? Surely a man fully grown can choose for himself."

The words came out sharper than she intended.

Before he could answer, Tyrek gave a loud snort and sat up. He rubbed his eyes and turned a sheepish smile on them.

"Did I miss anything?"

Uri shook his head. "Nothing important. Go back to sleep." Without a glance in Deborah's direction, he left.

She twisted around to watch him leave and was struck with a thought. Had he been about to confide in her?

Tyrek got to his feet and stretched. "I hope we do not march into battle the moment we arrive in Hamath. We will need rest after a four-day journey." His mouth stretched wide in a yawn. "At this moment I do not think I could lift a pebble, much less wield a sword."

She tilted her head to one side to study him. He was not handsome, like Uri, but a pleasing appearance was not a consideration when judging the character of a man. What admirable qualities did Tyrek possess? Was he honest? Dependable? Hardworking?

"Do you own a sword?" she asked.

He shook his head. "I hope to borrow a bow and quiver when we arrive. I am a passable archer, though I...lost mine before I left Jericho."

How did one lose a bow? A few possibilities occurred to her. Perhaps it was stolen while he lay in a drunken stupor. Or perhaps he traded it for wine.

"Why are you here, Tyrek?"

He looked startled at the question. Then his features softened, and he became thoughtful.

"You would like to hear me say I am zealous to see our people delivered from the Canaanites," he said in a low voice. "Or that I am an impassioned follower of Yahweh."

He fell silent. Questions erupted in Deborah's mind, but she held her tongue and waited for him to continue.

"The truth is less admirable," he admitted. "I would rather go to war than spend another day bent over a spinning, lifeless lump of clay, trying to fashion something usable with fingers that are not suited for the work."

At least he gave an honest answer. Compassion welled in her soul. Perhaps his wayward behavior was not due to rebellion, as so many assumed. Perhaps he had not yet found the role Yahweh intended, one to motivate him and give him peace.

"What else are you good at, Tyrek?" she asked. "What activity sparks your passion and stirs you to action?"

He responded in an offhand manner. "Let us hope it is soldiering."

When he had wandered in the direction Uri had taken, Deborah again leaned back against the bundles, disappointed. Perhaps Yahweh would use this conflict to reveal Tyrek's purpose. Despite his glib answer, she devoutly hoped it was not soldiering.

CHAPTER TWENTY-THREE

Deborah found travel the second day less arduous than the first. Eliakim did not set an easier pace, but her muscles fell into the previous day's rhythm quickly. She took the donkey's lead, freeing Lappidoth to circle through the men, asking about their families, their work, and their lives in Benjamin. Deborah prayed that these men, whose commitment to Yahweh's holy war could not be questioned, would settle her husband's doubts.

She, too, spoke with their fellow travelers. By ones and twos they fell in beside her, curious about her past and how a woman had become so wise in Torah. She told the story of her upbringing and hiding behind the curtains at the tabernacle to listen to the priests.

One man asked, "My abba taught me Torah from birth, and I know the holy writings well. Yet you are different. How did you become wise in the ways of Yahweh?"

She laughed and said, "Is anyone wise in the ways of Yahweh, man or woman? His ways are not ours, His thoughts beyond human wisdom."

The man persisted. "I have heard your judgments on the various conflicts and disputes presented to you. From where do these judgments come?"

The question surprised her. "From Yahweh, undoubtedly. He is the Source of all wisdom." Seeing he wanted more, she attempted an explanation. "When presented with a question, answers rise from inside me. Here, and here." She placed a hand on her stomach, and then on her chest.

Awe crept into his voice. "You hear the voice of Yahweh."

"Not always His voice," she said. "It is more like"—she searched for a description—"like knowledge that comes from beyond what I know myself." With a laugh at the inadequate description, she confessed, "Many times I am surprised at the words that fall from my lips."

She repeated variations of the same conversation several times throughout the day.

They traveled in small groups of three or four, sometimes forced to walk single file through heavily forested areas. At other times they were able to spread out across open plains. They splashed across streams and picked their way across rocky terrain while the sun traveled from their right arms to their left.

In the afternoon of the second day, Deborah found herself placed in the middle of the procession, with as many travelers in front of her as behind. When next Lappidoth caught up with her, she peered sideways at him.

"Did you arrange this?" She gestured to the men in front and then behind.

He did not deny it. "This place is the most secure. If we are attacked from any direction, you will be protected."

Though his concern touched her, her heart ached at the thought that worries for her safety plagued him.

"I am in Yahweh's hands," she said. "He will see me safely to Hamath."

"And then what?" He turned to her, his gaze piercing. "Will He see you home again? Will He protect you during the battle? Men die at war, Deborah. Has Yahweh promised that you will not?"

To that she had no ready answer. Only once had she inquired of Yahweh if she and those with whom she traveled would all journey home together when the war was accomplished. The next moment a deep sadness filled her, and she knew that some would not. Even some she would come to care about.

To Lappidoth, she said, "When Yahweh told Noah to build the ark, he obeyed. When He told Abram, 'Go from your country and your kindred and your father's house to the land that I will show you,' Abram went. Can we do less than they when Yahweh tells us to go?"

He fell silent, his expression thoughtful. Then someone from behind called his name, and he left to join them.

A realization had awakened in her as she walked toward an unknown future. Yahweh had given her life, and it was His to take. But to hear that would cause Lappidoth even more distress, so she held her tongue.

Yahweh, grant my husband the assurance You have given me. Give him peace.

They stopped well before sundown east of a town called Tizrah. Eliakim dispatched men to buy fresh bread and vegetables if there were any to be had. Though only two days had passed since their journey began and Deborah's supplies were still plentiful, she saw the wisdom in saving the more durable food. They did not know what would be available to them when they reached Hamath, when ten thousand men had arrived before them.

"Let us have a fire tonight," she told Lappidoth. "And I intend to roll out my mat to sleep on. Last night's grass was soft, but it made my skin itch."

Nodding, he called for Tyrek. "Come with me to gather wood."

The two joined others with the same goal and headed in the direction of a thick stand of trees not far ahead. Deborah knelt to untie their sleeping mats.

"Look here. Do you see what you did?"

Gersham's angry voice drew her attention. He and Uri had stopped a short distance away. She looked in that direction in time to see Gersham grab a pack on their donkey's back and give it a shake. A long-handled axe fell to the ground. He snatched it up and shook it in the air.

"Do you not know how to tie a rope, boy? We could have lost my axe along the way. Would you have me face the Canaanites without a weapon?"

Deborah winced at the fury in his shout. Uri stood before him with his head bowed low. Several men in the vicinity paused to stare at the father and son.

"How could I have spawned such a useless fool?" Gersham tossed the axe at Uri, who caught it by the metal head before it hit the ground a second time. "Do better tomorrow." He stomped away.

When Uri lifted his head, everyone in the area returned to their tasks and avoided his eyes. Deborah focused on untying the knotted fabric around a bundle, her heart aching. No matter how angry their children made Lappidoth, not once had she ever heard him belittle them or even raise his voice.

"Forgive me for intruding, but can you spare a scrap of cloth?"

She looked up to find Uri standing beside her. He extended his hand, and she saw blood seeping from a wound across his palm.

"I do not want to bleed on our bundles trying to find a bandage."

Deborah understood what he did not say. After witnessing Gersham's anger over a loosely tied knot, she could not imagine how he might react to blood on his belongings.

She nodded and untied the pack containing their food supplies. From there she removed the cloth wrapping two small loaves—they would be stale in another day anyway—and also withdrew a small jar of honey.

"Sit here," she instructed Uri, who sank to the ground in front of her. "Give me your hand."

She uncorked her water skin, washed the wound, and then pressed around it with gentle fingers.

"It is not deep," she told him, and removed the waxed cloth covering the honey.

"Hardly a scratch," he said. Then he jerked his hand away. "What are you doing with that?"

"Have you never heard of covering a wound with honey?" she asked, amused at his display of nerves. She took his hand again and tipped the jar to drizzle a thin stream of the thick golden liquid over the cut. "Our ancestors learned it while in Egypt. Honey not only tastes good, it has healing properties as well. The Egyptians also use grease to seal a wound, but I did not think to bring that."

She ripped a strip of cloth from the bread covering. After folding the remainder, she placed it over his palm and tied it tightly. Then she released his hand and sat back.

"When Yahweh told our ancestors He would bring them to a land flowing with milk and honey, I like to think He meant a land of rest and of healing."

"Milk does help us sleep." Then he flexed his bandaged hand. "Thank you. I...suppose you heard?" He jerked his head over his shoulder, toward his and Gersham's belongings.

She did not trust herself to speak but answered with a nod.

"He does not mean those things," Uri told her, still staring at the bandage. "My brothers say he was kinder before..."

"Before your imma died?" she asked.

It was his turn not to answer.

"I remember your imma." He looked up to meet her eyes. "Lilah was already a mother twice over when I arrived as Lappidoth's wife. I did not know her well, but I remember she laughed a lot. I saw her on market days, with a child on one hip and pulling another by the hand, always smiling and offering a kind word to others."

"She smelled like cinnamon," he said, his voice distant as though lost in a memory. "I remember cinnamon. But not much else."

Deborah spoke in a quiet voice. "Lilah honored Yahweh and kept His mitzvah."

Pain flashed across his features. Then it was gone, replaced by a wooden expression that twisted Deborah's heart in her chest. At least the irritating smirk she was accustomed to seeing proved that he felt something. At that moment he looked as if he had discarded all emotion, like she would discard a piece of rotting fruit.

He stood and lifted his hand. "Thank you." He left without waiting for an answer.

She covered the honey and secured the waxed cloth in place, her mind on their conversation. How old had Uri been when his imma died? Not more than four or five years. How terrible it would have been to be raised in a home with an angry, bitter father and two domineering older brothers. She could almost weep when she considered—

She jerked upright.

Yahweh, what is this? That is Uri, *the idolater who desires my daughter.*

A rush of compassion rose up inside her, so strong it nearly took her breath. In an instant, she knew, without doubt, the Source of the emotion. Yahweh Himself grieved for the young boy Uri had been, and for what his pain and loss had formed him to be.

This is why You drew him to my family. So he may learn that You love him, and that You were not the cause of his pain.

How that message would be delivered, Deborah did not know. Only that it would. And soon. During this journey.

"Deborah!"

The shout pulled her out of her thoughts. She looked up to find Oded leading a group of perhaps ten strangers in her direction.

"These people are from Tizrah," he told her when they drew near. "They have heard of the woman warrior, and of Deborah's Palm, and have come to hear you speak of your vision in the stars."

Woman warrior? Her first instinct was to laugh at the idea of wielding a weapon in battle. She swallowed the urge and instead smiled her greeting at the newcomers.

"I am humbled that my vision is known here, in Manasseh. The vision was mine, but the message is Yahweh's."

"Tell us, Prophetess," said one of the men.

He sat on the grass, and those with him did as well. Oded, too, sat with them, though he had heard her describe the vision and Yahweh calling the people of Israel to war. She began to talk, to describe not only what her eyes saw but then how the magnitude of Yahweh's plan brought her to her knees in awe. She told them of hearing Barak's name and knowing he was Yahweh's chosen commander of the army that would deliver them from oppression. Of their meeting, and his efforts to call together ten thousand men.

By the time she finished, her audience had grown to include every man in their company, even though they had heard her speak before on that same topic. When she fell silent, a vibrant energy seemed to hover over the listeners.

Then a man from Tizrah stood. "I will go." His voice carried to the edges of their camp. "I will answer Yahweh's call."

Immediately two others joined him, and then others. Within minutes all the men were on their feet, shouting their devotion and dedication to Yahweh.

Her gaze was drawn to a lone figure standing well away from the others, his arms folded, scanning the crowd from beneath unkempt eyebrows. As she watched, Gersham turned his back and walked away.

She searched for Uri and found him on the opposite side of the shouting men. He stood with his arms dangling at his sides, watching his abba leave.

CHAPTER TWENTY-FOUR

The experience at Tizrah repeated many times, and their number increased. Twice they encountered men on the road, blocking their way and asking to hear from the woman prophet. The third night they camped at Jezreel in Issachar. There, they were met by a group of women who had been told of their approach.

"Many of the men of our town have gone ahead of you to join the army in Hamath," an elderly woman said to Deborah. "Will you tell us about the stars?"

The town had prepared a feast to honor them, and while her traveling companions ate, she did as the woman requested. When the group left the next morning, they went with fresh foodstuffs and many spoken blessings.

Lappidoth stayed close to her that day. Issachar's northern border lay only a few miles from the southernmost shore of the Sea of Galilee. To the east was the land of the Arameans, through which Sisera had been known to send companies of his men to pillage Israelite farms and towns.

"Keep watch," he instructed Tyrek, who walked just ahead of them.

The young man had purchased a bow in Jezreel, and he held it in his hand as they walked. On his back he carried a quiver full of arrows.

Everywhere Deborah looked she saw weapons in evidence. Swords, axes, bows, and spears that she supposed had been previously packed on donkeys now protruded from packs above men's heads or dangled at their sides, readily available at the first hint of danger. Some, like Gersham, even carried their weapons in their hands. Few spoke, and those who did kept their voices low.

As they neared the border of Issachar, they came upon a wide valley. Deborah's eyes were drawn to an enormous hill that rose high from the flat land surrounding it. Though the day was warm, a chill crept up her spine and spread down her arms. She was dimly aware that her feet had stopped moving, her gaze fixed on the mountain that seemed to stand guard over the valley.

Lappidoth peered at her, deep creases in his brow. "What is it?"

She shook her head, her mouth so dry she could not speak. Those traveling in their immediate vicinity also halted, and Oded approached.

Seeing where she looked, he said, "We are at the southeast edge of the Jezreel Valley." He nodded at the mound. "That is Mount Tabor."

Deborah cleared her throat. "It resembles my hill at home, only so much larger."

A silent laugh blasted through her husband's nose. "And much steeper. To climb to the top of that every day, you would need the strength of a giant."

Oded peered at her, his eyes narrowed. "What is it? What do you see?"

She was aware that he, and those in their immediate vicinity, waited for her answer.

Tearing her eyes away, she gave her head a quick shake. "Nothing. It is an impressive sight."

She did not say what she felt in the depths of her soul. That this was the place Yahweh had chosen for the battle with the Canaanites.

Midday on the fourth day of their journey, they came upon the Israelite army just south of Hamath. For the second time that day, Deborah stood still with her jaw dangling.

"Ten thousand men is…" A description failed her. "A lot."

The company stretched to the east, west, and north as far as she could see. Tents had been erected everywhere, a mishmash of sizes and shapes, though they were all set at even distances apart in orderly lines.

"It resembles the area around the tabernacle at Passover," Lappidoth said. "Only more orderly."

When Eliakim at the front of their group reached the edge of the encampment, he was met by a line of grim-faced men, each with a sword or spear held at the ready. He and one of them exchanged words, but from her place in the center Deborah could hear nothing.

Oded came up beside her. "You should be at Eliakim's side."

Startled, she looked up at him.

"He is right," Lappidoth said before she could reject the idea. The smile he gave her was tender, personal. "The time has come for Deborah the Judge."

She searched his face, fearful that she would see reluctance or regret. Instead, she found admiration shining in his eyes.

Straightening to her full height, she tossed her head and nodded at Oded. He gestured for her to precede him but followed close on her heels with Lappidoth at his side.

"We have brought her with us."

She heard Eliakim's words as she drew near. He half turned to search for her.

"I am here." She looked at the guard who stood before him. "Send a message to Barak son of Abinoam. Tell him Deborah has arrived from Ephraim accompanied by men who are faithful to Yahweh and committed to serving Him."

The guard's head turned as he looked over the new arrivals, and then his gaze settled once more on her. A fierce zeal glinted in his eyes.

"Then it is nearly time." He awarded her a respectful half bow. "Come. I will take you to Barak."

When he turned, the men standing before him parted to let him through. Deborah followed, aware that Eliakim fell in beside Oded and Lappidoth, and a string of others after them.

Her escort led them between the sea of tents. Word spread quickly, and soon soldiers lined the path they walked, all of them watching her. Some wore smiles, and some faces were set with an intense determination. She saw them from the corners of her eyes, which she kept fixed ahead. Whispers of *prophetess* and *judge* reached her as she passed.

After they passed what seemed like hundreds, if not thousands, of men, their destination came into view. A large canopy easily the size of her rooftop at home had been stretched over a frame of poles, some of which were planted in the ground. A low table rested beneath it, with ten men gathered around its rough wooden surface. When they drew near, the men turned.

Barak stood and his head nearly touched the canopy. She had forgotten how tall he was.

His gaze fixed on hers. "You made good time. Faster than I hoped."

"And you gathered ten thousand men faster than I expected," she replied, then admitted, "though I cannot deny that I counted each day from the moment you left."

He looked behind her, and she turned to follow his gaze. The men who had traveled with her had taken up their weapons and followed.

She faced Barak once more. "Word of Yahweh's favor has spread. We number less than a hundred, not many in comparison, but every one is eager to fight for Barak, the commander of Yahweh's army."

His lips twitched. "I suspect they are eager to fight for Deborah." He dipped his head. "As I am." Without waiting for a response, he gestured to those who had been seated around the table with him and who now stood. "These men will lead companies of a thousand each into battle." To them he said, "This is Deborah, the voice of Yahweh."

She met and held the gaze of each, nodding to acknowledge them.

Barak raised his voice to address to the men lined up behind her. "Men of Israel, be welcomed and blessed. I commend you for your dedication to Yahweh, and for your bravery." He turned his head. "Phineas." One of the leaders stepped to his side. "Take charge of the newcomers. Assign them where their skills and weapons are needed."

Lappidoth stepped to Deborah's side. "Appoint the others as you see fit. I will not leave her side."

A wide smile broke out on Barak's face. "Welcome, my friend." To those standing behind him he said, "This is Lappidoth, the husband of Deborah."

Though Deborah kept her face impassive, inwardly she cringed. In all her years not once had she heard a man introduced as the husband of his wife. She risked a sideways glance. Lappidoth stood tall and dignified, perhaps even a touch proud.

Barak addressed them both. "I have a tent ready for you. Come with me."

They followed, Lappidoth now at her side, matching her step for step. They had not gone far when they came upon two tents, larger than the ones lined in rows throughout the grounds. He stopped at the first and pulled a panel of fabric aside for them to enter. She ducked inside, and they followed.

The smell of fresh straw struck her, the source obvious. A wide pallet occupied much of the meager space. Beside it someone had placed a lamp and a sealed jug she assumed to contain oil. Those were the only contents.

She gestured to the pallet. "I did not expect luxury in an army camp."

"Enjoy it," Barak told her. "You will find very few comforts here. Even necessities are likely to become rare if the war stretches more than a few weeks."

"How are the men?" Lappidoth asked. "Are they prepared to face the Canaanites?"

"Some are. Most have never seen battle." Barak spread his legs apart and clasped his hands behind his back. "We have conducted training. Weapon strategies, close combat methods, attack tactics, and the like." He scowled and admitted, "I would feel better with months or even years to prepare, but the time grows short."

"How so?

"A gathering of ten thousand men cannot go unnoticed. My spies brought news two days past that King Jabin has received reports that Israel is amassing an army. He has instructed Sisera to gather his chariots and soldiers in Harosheth of the Gentiles and to prepare them for battle."

Lappidoth shook his head. "I do not know the place."

"It is near Meggido, on the shores of the Great Sea. Perhaps two days' march from here, longer with heavy chariots." Barak set his jaw. "I do not wish to fight them here. That is the debate we were having around the command table when you arrived.

We must choose the location with care to ensure we have an advantage when we meet Sisera."

"I know where the battle will take place," Deborah said.

They both turned to her with nearly identical startled expressions.

"You will take your army to Mount Tabor in the Valley of Jezreel." Though she knew nothing about wars and attacks, she spoke with confidence. "We will make camp on the mountain. Yahweh will draw Sisera to you there."

Barak's eyes lit. "When? How long do we have?"

She shook her head. "I have told you everything Yahweh has revealed to me."

"Thus far." He grasped Lappidoth's arm, his excitement evident. "Mount Tabor is an ideal location. I can plan a battle strategy now that I know the place. I must tell the others. We will break camp at sunrise and make haste to the Jezreel Valley." To her he said, "We must know the timing. You will inquire of Yahweh?"

At her nod, he left the tent.

Deborah spoke in a low voice to Lappidoth. "I do not know the time," she said. "But of one thing I am certain. It will not be long."

CHAPTER TWENTY-FIVE

Night found Deborah and Lappidoth standing outside their tent, looking out over the camp. A nearly round moon cast its white light over the tents that spread out in all directions. Hundreds of fires dotted the encampment in an even pattern. Deborah had been escorted down row after even row by Barak and Lappidoth, and asked to repeat the story of her vision so often she lost count.

"What do you intend to do with that?"

She pointed at the sword Barak had provided when he discovered that Lappidoth had nothing with which to guard her but determination and bravery. To her knowledge her husband had never held a sword, much less wielded one.

He glanced at the heavy weapon leaning against the side of their tent. "One of Barak's captains intends to instruct me in its use beginning tomorrow." His brow wrinkled with uncertainty, he lifted his head to look toward the command tent where Barak and his appointed leaders sat in the lamplight, going over every detail of the upcoming conflict. "I am going to ask Barak if it is absolutely necessary." Extending his hand, he asked, "Do you want to come with me?"

"You go. I am tired and eager to stretch out in comfort on a soft bed instead of the hard ground."

He placed a kiss upon her forehead. "I will return shortly."

When he had gone, she ducked inside the tent. Only a trace of moonlight shone through the narrow opening above her. She did not light the lamp, nor did she lay on the cushioned bed. The day had taken its toll, and she longed to be alone for a few minutes to pray.

She fell to her knees, closed her eyes, and lifted her hands. How she missed her palm tree and the peaceful solitude she always found there. A place of silence could not be found in the midst of ten thousand men, though she did her best to block out the voices drifting through the fabric of the tent.

"Yahweh, cover these men, the children of Israel, with Your protection," she prayed. "Return them to their mothers, their wives, and their children unharmed." At the mention of children, sorrow stabbed at her heart. How she missed hers. "Watch over Tivon, Sabra, and Doda Yocheved," she whispered. "Guard them and preserve their lives until You bring us together again."

Barak's request pressed against her mind. "Yahweh, my King, Your army is gathered. Your people await Your guidance. What shall I tell them? When will we march to the place You have revealed to me?"

Her tongue fell silent. She reached outward with her spirit, longing to sense the Presence that would bring peace to her soul. A tendril of despair threatened to invade her thoughts. Where was Yahweh? Why could she not hear Him?

"I have given my life into Your hands." Though she held her eyes tightly shut, tears leaked through to wet her cheeks. "I have left everything behind. My home. My family. Do not desert me now."

Rest.

The word washed through her, releasing tension from her muscles and banishing her worries. A heavy fatigue crept over her, and she crawled to the bed, tears of relief now flowing unchecked.

"You have not forgotten me," she whispered in the moment before sleep overtook her.

By the sixth hour the following day, the army had covered several miles. At Barak's insistence, Deborah and Lappidoth walked at his side in front of the entire procession. The hilly terrain made travel difficult, especially for the large number of men and pack animals. Whenever she looked back, the company spread into the distance farther than she could see.

They crested a hill, and Barak came to a halt.

"Why have we stopped?" Deborah asked.

In answer he merely pointed. When she looked up, her breath caught in her chest.

Before them stretched the Jezreel Valley, green, fertile, and flat. Though she had traveled through it only two days before, on her way to Hamath, from this angle the plain looked wider. Few trees dotted the landscape. Rising from the valley stood Mount Tabor, looking from her vantage point like a pottery bowl upturned in the center of her worktable.

Barak swung his arm to the right. "The Kishon River is there. It flows to the northwest and empties into the sea."

Sunlight glinted off a ribbon of water that wound through the valley on the far side of the mountain.

Lappidoth shielded his eyes and squinted in that direction. "It looks more like a narrow stream than a river."

"At the moment it does," Barak agreed. "But when the rains fall it becomes impassible."

"A shame the rains have stopped, then," Deborah commented. "You said the encampment of Sisera's army lay to the west, by the sea. We might have been able to use a flooded river to our advantage."

Barak turned an amused grin toward her. "Well spoken, Prophetess. I shall make a warrior of you yet."

Though Deborah laughed at the idea, she noted Lappidoth's disapproving scowl.

"We will make the foot of the mountain in good time," Barak told them both. "From there we will take a small company of men and climb to the top." He looked down at her. "You will come and ask Yahweh to show us where to establish our camp."

Without waiting for an answer, he strode forward, down the slope toward the valley below.

Lappidoth frowned at his back. "He speaks orders to you as he would to one of his soldiers."

Touched by his concern, she laid a calming hand on his arm. "That is why we are here." She spoke quietly, so her voice would not carry down the hill in either direction. "He doubts himself." She stared after Barak. "If only his faith was stronger, he would hear Yahweh's voice on his own."

Her husband's smile became tender. "Not everyone has the capacity for limitless faith like yours."

"Limitless?" She laughed aloud. "Even the faith of our forefathers had limits. Did not Moses strike the rock when Yahweh told him only to speak?"

He nodded his agreement. "If not limitless, then at least immense." His gaze fixed in the distance, and he grinned. "My wife has faith the size of Mount Tabor."

Chuckling together, they followed Barak down the hill.

They marched across the Jezreel Valley. The mountain appeared to grow as they neared. Deborah could hardly take her eyes off it. Inside her a truth took root and grew as the rounded peak drew and held her gaze. The grassy slopes of Mount Tabor that loomed before her would soon drink the blood of men, both Israelite and Canaanite.

When they reached the foot of the mountain, Barak called a halt and sent for two of his captains.

"Take ten men each and circle the mount," he told them, pointing in each direction. "Search for the easiest route to the pinnacle. That is the direction Sisera will take." He placed a hand on each man's shoulder. "May Yahweh give you the eyes of eagles."

They left, followed by their men.

Deborah found a flat rock not far away and perched on it to rest her feet. Lappidoth sat beside her and together they watched Barak weave through his resting army, pausing often to exchange a few words with the men he encountered.

Those who occupied the area around Deborah maintained a polite distance, though many of them stole glances at her from veiled eyes. They looked on her with varying degrees of reverence and awe. To be expected, she knew, since Barak identified her often and loudly as Israel's judge and the mouth-piece of Yahweh.

"I feel as though I am on display," she said as she stood. "Let us walk and escape the stares."

Lappidoth laughed. "If that is your aim, you will have to hide in a cave."

But he joined her. Together they headed west, following after the scouts who had been sent in that direction. Before long they reached the end of the company. From that vantage point she could see the that their number stretched far into the valley.

"If this is ten thousand men," she said, "I cannot fathom what forty thousand will look like."

She did not expect an answer, and he gave none. Instead he peered at a small cluster of men who had separated them-selves from the rest.

"That looks like Tyrek," he said.

Since arriving at Hamath, Deborah had not seen many of those who accompanied them from Ephraim. Oded had sought her out at sunrise, as they packed their belongings and once again loaded them on the back of their donkey. He told her that Eliakim had been placed in charge of several hundred men, including Gersham and Uri.

As they neared Tyrek and the others, she saw what had drawn them off to one side. Ophira's brother stood beside five others, each holding a bow with an arrow held at the ready. One man, clearly their leader, paced behind the line, giving instructions in an even voice.

"Relax your grip. Use your fingers to steady the arrow. Do not use your arm to draw the string. Pull from your back. When the string touches your nose, align the arrow with the target."

He caught sight of them and gave a start when he recognized Deborah. He bowed his head to acknowledge her, then returned his attention to the archers standing before him.

A good distance in front of them stood a lone tree. Was that their target? To her, the trunk looked no wider than her thigh.

"When you are ready, let the string slide from your fingers."

The sound of arrows whizzed through the air. One struck the ground a short distance away, and a frustrated cry tore from the throat of the man closest to them. Four more overshot the tree. Only one hit the tree with an audible *thunk*.

The man standing next to Tyrek shouted, "Success!"

Tyrek rounded on him. "Your eyes deceive you. I hit the target, not you."

Deborah glanced at Lappidoth, amazed. She had never heard him speak in a tone so amiable, so full of good humor. He sounded lighter, more relaxed.

The two raced to the tree and bent close to inspect the arrow. Then Tyrek threw his hands in the air and shouted a victory cry. His companion wandered off after the others to search for his arrow.

Turning, Tyrek caught sight of them, and a wide grin broke out on his face. He approached at a run.

"Did you see that?" he asked.

"Impressive," Lappidoth told him, and Tyrek's chest swelled.

The instructor strode forward to thump Tyrek's back. "The boy's a fine archer, with a sure eye and a steady hand." He looked toward the others and then shouted, "You there! Amos. Open your eyes, you blind clod. It is right in front of your feet." He stomped away.

Tyrek turned to Deborah. "I am no good at pottery, but put a bow in my hand and watch what I can do."

She could not help but return his smile. "Perhaps you will become a mighty hunter. You will bring meat to your family's table and coins into their purses."

His smile dimmed. "I do not intend to return to Ephraim." He glanced at Lappidoth. "When we have rid ourselves of the Canaanites, there are still the Arameans who are kept at bay by their fear of Sisera's iron chariots. The people here, in the north, will need swordsmen and bowmen so they may live in peace and in safety."

Dismayed, Deborah peered into his eyes. "But what of your family? Your sister, who will fret over *your* safety?"

His gaze softened at the mention of his sister. "Ophira knows my struggles more than anyone else. She will understand if you explain it to her, and I think she will be happy for me."

Behind him the instructor bellowed. "Once more. Line up, and this time heed my words!"

Tyrek threw a glance over his shoulder. "I must go. You will speak to Ophira for me, will you not?"

How could she refuse in the face of such enthusiasm? "I will."

With a final grin at Lappidoth, he raced back to his friends.

"I do not believe Ophira will receive the news as easily as he might think," she said, watching him go.

"A man must choose for himself the path he walks." Lappidoth took her arm. "Come. We are distracting them."

She realized she was the focus of attention of several of the archers. In a moment their brusque teacher would notice, and he did not seem the type to tolerate distractions. They turned and headed back toward the front to wait for Barak's scouts to return.

The men returned. Deborah remained seated on the rock while Barak conferred with the troops he had sent out. She tilted her head back, her eyes searching the dense trees that covered the slopes of Mount Tabor as far as she could see. From the other side of the valley she had seen what looked like open land at the top, but now she only saw trees. Hundreds, if not thousands, of them. It would take them the better part of a day to pick their way through them.

Barak finished his conversation and approached her, his stride long and purposeful.

"My men have found the path of ascent," he told them. "A wide swath of land on the southwestern slope with little growth. An easy march for an army." His face became grim. "And for chariots."

At the mention of a pathway, a warm sensation flared deep in Deborah's chest. A feeling of rightness spread through her.

"We passed to the east when we arrived," Lappidoth said. "All we saw was more of this." He swept a hand upward, indicating the heavily forested mountainside.

Barak nodded. "I will dispatch a few men to Harosheth-Haggoyim while the rest of us advance to the summit and set up camp. We will take the high ground and force Sisera to climb to meet us." He peered into Deborah's face. "Does this plan meet with your approval, Prophetess?"

Without a moment's hesitation, she got to her feet and nodded. "May the God of our forefathers, of Abraham, Isaac, and Jacob, go before us to prepare the way."

They found the trail exactly as the scouts had described it. A wide strip of ground, as if someone had carved a road through the trees. The land lay bare before them, covered with only a smattering of yellowed grasses. Barak paused only for a moment, his eyes moving as he scanned the area ahead of them, and then began the upward march. Lappidoth extended his hand, and she took it. Together they began the upward trek.

They reached the summit while the sun still hovered above the western horizon.

Barak stopped at the end of a wide clearing, but Deborah passed him, drawn by an urge she did not understand and could not resist. The land continued to slant upward, though gently. Her legs barely noticed the incline. She did not stop until she reached the center of the open area.

Turning in a slow circle, she noted the forest's edge on the three sides, though not as dense here as below. Behind her, Barak and Lappidoth stood at the head of a line of men that reached almost all the way to the flatlands below. Beyond them, to the south and west, she traced a path through the valley, across the narrow stream of the Kishon River, and beyond that, to the edge of yet another forest. Soon she would see Sisera's army emerge from between those trees and charge toward her. The thought did not frighten her, as it might once have done. The time for fear was over. This was Yahweh's war, and she stood at the head of Yahweh's army. Her life—the lives of all of them—were in His hands.

Lifting her head, she called across the distance to Barak. "Have your men make camp. We will stay here and wait for Yahweh's guidance."

CHAPTER TWENTY-SIX

Unable to bear breathing the stale air one moment longer, Deborah escaped the confines of her tent. Lappidoth had left to train with the swordsmen an hour past. Though she had no desire to pick up a weapon, she envied his chance to put his hands and his mind to good use.

For three days they had camped on Mount Tabor with no word from Yahweh. She grew weary of Barak's questions and the frustration that darkened his features when she could not give him the answers he wanted. A pair of his spies returned two days past with news that Sisera's army increased by the hour, but thus far they had seen no sign of movement.

Though she managed to avoid attracting Barak's attention, she drew the gaze of the men as she strode down the mountain in search of her husband. They stopped whatever activity they were engaged in to watch her, and often to exchange a few words. She had grown accustomed to their awed stares. Some knelt before her to ask for a blessing. Those she gave freely, acutely aware that some of those she blessed would not see the end of the coming war.

Partway down the mountain she heard the sound of metal on metal from behind a sparse stand of trees. Experienced warriors had begun conducting their training amid the trees, reasoning, Lappidoth told her, that it would be to their advantage to draw their enemy into the heavily forested area where chariots could not go and horses only slowly. Turning in the direction her ears detected, she followed the sounds to a small clearing, only a fraction the size of the one at the mount's summit. Pairs of men were scattered about, swinging their swords at one another with what looked like deadly force. A stern-faced man paced between them with his hands folded behind his back, shouting instructions to be heard above the clashing of their weapons. Other men stood in a loose circle around them, well out of the way, watching.

"Do not stand in one place," the instructor roared. "Your feet are as much a weapon as your sword."

She scanned the faces of the participants, relieved when she did not see her husband. He must be practicing elsewhere. Hopefully with a less violent opponent than these. She started to go but stopped when she recognized one of the fighters. Uri. As she watched, his opponent raised his weapon and brought it crashing down. Her breath halted in her chest, certain Uri was about to suffer a devastating injury. Instead, he planted a foot behind him and spun away. The man's sword hit the ground, and a cheer went up from those watching.

"That is what I mean," the instructor shouted. "Predict where the sword will strike, and move out of harm's way."

"Do not stop there, boy," shouted a familiar gruff voice. "Attack while he is off balance."

She looked to her left, where Gersham stood apart from the others with his arms folded across his chest. His eyes were mere slits as he watched his son.

Deborah had not seen either of them since they arrived at Hamath. The memory of his anger on the road, and Uri's excuses on his behalf, returned to her. She backed up into the trees so she would not distract the swordsmen and made her way to the other side of the clearing. When she stepped to Gersham's side, he acknowledged her with a quick glance before returning his attention to the action in the clearing.

"Uri is doing well," she said quietly.

He replied with a nearly inaudible grunt, which she took to mean he agreed.

"He looks like he has wielded a sword for years."

"He is quick-footed," Gersham admitted. Then his lip curled. "He is not as strong as his brothers."

"He is still young," she said. "He will grow stronger."

She could hardly believe the words had come from her. Here she stood, defending the young man who took pleasure in plaguing her, who never missed an opportunity to smirk at her teaching.

"If he does not get himself killed first," he said with a sneer.

His tone struck Deborah as sharply as one of the swords in the clearing. She had heard his son speak in a nearly identical tone many times.

"He is like you," she said. "At least, he tries to be."

His head jerked toward her. "He is the least of my sons like me."

"Perhaps he resembles Lilah then," she said quietly.

Pain flashed across his face. He looked away, in the direction of the exercise in the clearing, but his eyes were distant, unfocused, as if fixed on something only he could see. His silence stretched long, and Deborah regretted her comment. She had prodded a painful wound, one he was not willing to let her see.

When he spoke, it was in a soft voice, one she had never heard from him.

"Uri is the smartest of my sons." He did not look at her. "He is quick-witted, like his imma." He swallowed. "Like my Lilah."

She searched for soothing words, for something that would wipe the pain from his features. But anything she said would sound feeble, so she stilled her tongue.

"He has her looks as well," he said quietly. "Sometimes when he smiles, it is like Lilah is smiling through his eyes."

Still, Deborah said nothing. Her heart ached to see his features twisted with grief. *Yahweh, he needs Your peace.*

"I have been hard on him because of Lilah." His gaze remained fixed on Uri as he spoke. "There is a distance between us."

"Distances can be crossed."

He shook his head. "Not this one."

Words rose up from inside her. "Yahweh is accustomed to helping His people traverse great distances. Did He not part the Red Sea so our ancestors could cross safely to freedom?"

He did look at her then, his face an unreadable mask. She waited for his response, but he turned away and left the clearing without a word.

Deborah woke with a start to near total darkness. Where was she? Her brain struggled to throw off the cloying tendrils of sleep that dulled her thoughts. She extended a hand and felt her husband's warm body beside her.

Lappidoth stirred at her touch, but a moment later his breath returned to the deep, rhythmic pattern she had grown accustomed to during the years of their life together. She rolled to her side and felt the straw shift beneath her.

Her memory returned in a flash. She was on Mount Tabor, with ten thousand men spread out around her, ready to take up their weapons in honor of Yahweh.

Today would be the day. Her heart quickened and blood pulsed in her ears.

Rise! Today My people will utterly destroy the Canaanite army.

Though she knew the Voice sounded only in her head, her ears rang with the clarion call.

"Lappidoth!" She grabbed him with both hands and shook him awake. "We must waken Barak. Tell him to ready his men."

Fully alert in an instant, Lappidoth leaped from the bed. Her eyes grew accustomed to the darkness enough to see him snatch something from the corner and toss it in her direction.

"Put this on," he told her in a tone that brooked no argument, and then he hurried from the tent.

At Lappidoth's insistence, Barak had supplied her with battle armor. She protested. The army had been assembled so quickly there had been no time to find armor for most of the men.

"If they march into battle without, then so should I," she had argued.

To no avail. She did not know where they found protective garments to fit her, and Lappidoth refused to tell her.

In the dark, she slipped the heavy leather breastplate over her head and pulled the lacings tight. Greaves covered her shins, and a thick helmet sat snugly on her head. Her hair hung in a long plait down her back.

Voices reached her from outside as she secured her sandals. Barak's shouts to his men, and the roar of their voices in answer. Once dressed, she started to leave when her foot struck an object on the ground. Lappidoth had run out in such a hurry he'd left his sword behind. Were her stomach not full of tense knots, she might have found that humorous. But now was no time for humor. She seized the sword and looped the scabbard across one shoulder. It was lighter and shorter than some, a fact that had caused her silent anguish. The weapon would be of no use unless an enemy was upon them. She prayed Lappidoth would not be called upon to wield it at all.

Outside she found a flurry of orderly activity. Grim-faced men emerged from tents and hurried toward previously arranged places to join their assigned troops. She fell in with them, heading for the canopy where Barak and his trusted leaders met to plan their strategies.

"Deborah, over here." Ahead she saw an arm waving, and she veered toward Lappidoth.

"Barak has called for you," he told her when she joined him.

He grabbed her arm and pulled her forward. His fingers bit into her flesh, but she swallowed a protest and instead stretched her legs to match his pace.

When she stepped beneath the canopy where Barak stood with his trusted leaders, it was as if she entered an oasis. Outside, men rushed around in a frenzy of activity, but Barak stood tall and calm. Not until she drew near did she see the hard set of his jaw and the glint of iron in his eyes.

"What have you heard?" He searched her face. "What has Yahweh revealed to you?"

Three days past she might have shrunk from the intensity in his voice. Even last night she might have stammered her response. But the time for shrinking and stammering was gone. She straightened to her full height, fortified by an overwhelming a boldness that could only come from a Source outside herself.

"The day has arrived." Her voice carried beyond the canopy, bolstered not by volume but by a fierce certainty that she spoke the words of Yahweh. Activity in the vicinity ceased as men paused to listen. Beside her, Lappidoth watched her without blinking.

"Before the sun sets you will see the power of the One who spoke the earth into being."

A shout from the back of the listeners reached her. "Give us a blessing, Deborah, Judge of Israel."

"Yes, Prophetess," Barak said. "Give us your blessing."

Your blessing, my King, not mine. Give these men Your blessing.

She raised her arms, her palms facing those gathered before her. As one, they sank to their knees. Barak, too, knelt, as did the others beneath the canopy. Even Lappidoth dropped to the ground, his face alight. She might have protested but for the certitude that her husband knelt not before his wife but before Yahweh's chosen.

The words of the blessing rose up from deep inside. "May Yahweh cause the enemies who rise up against us to be struck down. May the Holy One, King of the universe, preserve and rescue our fighting men from every trouble and distress. May He deliver our enemies into your hands and crown you with victory. For it is Yahweh, the God of Abraham, Isaac, and Jacob, who goes with you into battle."

As the last word left her lips, a man dashed through those kneeling before her. He ran forward and fell at her feet, panting heavily.

"They come. The Canaanites." He stabbed a finger wildly toward the west. "Even now they are marching toward us. They will be here within an hour."

Deborah turned to Barak. "Rise. Go. This day Yahweh will give Sisera into your hands."

He leaped up and whirled to face his trusted leaders. "Assemble your companies. Send them into the trees and across the trails as they have been trained. Listen for the trumpet's blast, and do not move until you hear it."

They scattered, and the flurry of activity resumed as men ran to obey.

Deborah lowered her hands, and Lappidoth took them in his. He lifted them to his lips and gently kissed her fingertips. Then, with a grin, he lifted the scabbard from her shoulder and slung it across his own.

"You make an inspiring sight for the men, Warrior Woman, but allow me the honor of protecting my wife."

He gave her the wink that never failed to thrill her.

CHAPTER TWENTY-SEVEN

The sun rose and proved the scout's words true. Deborah stood at the summit of Mount Tabor, Barak on her right and Lappidoth on her left. Behind them, two hundred Israelites stood at the ready, holding whatever weapons they had at their disposal. The trumpeter also stood behind, waiting for the command to sound the charge. Before them stretched the Jezreel Valley, awash with golden light. Thousands of Canaanites had crossed the river already, and still their number stretched far into the forest beyond. Their chariots splashed across as she watched, a fearsome number of them.

"Will they wait until the entire army has forded the Kishon before attacking?" Lappidoth asked.

Barak shook his head. "Sisera will amass half of his men on this side. Not until his army outnumbers ours two to one will he march."

"He knows the number of our men?" Deborah asked.

"As well as we know his."

She glanced up at him. "Will you attack while the numbers are not so strong against us? Before twenty thousand cross over?"

Barak's mouth pressed into a hard line, his eyes not moving from the scene before him. "We will wait."

Minutes stretched long, and Deborah lost count. Had it been one hour since she spoke the blessing, or three? The bulk of Israel's ten thousand warriors filled the wide trail, their weapons held at the ready, their bodies tense. Yet they barely stretched to the midway point of the mountain. The company behind her shifted from foot to foot, waiting for their commander to give the word.

"Look there."

Barak pointed to a large group of Canaanite foot soldiers that stood apart from the others. One of the chariots broke away from the others and rode toward them. A man stood on the platform suspended between two wheels, pulled by a pair of horses.

"It is Sisera," Barak said with gravel in his voice.

"How do you know?" From the distance Deborah could make out no details.

"I know."

She did not doubt him.

"He will divide that company and send them to engage us, half up each side of the trail."

"Through the trees?" Lappidoth asked. "But that is where some of our men are placed."

Still Barak did not take his eyes from the scene below them. "That is why he will do it. It is what I would do."

Deborah watched as Barak's prediction proved true. The group standing before the lone chariot divided. Half crossed in front of the main force and took up a position opposite the others. The chariot circled and rode to the center, and though she could not hear, she knew Sisera was addressing his army. The mass of Canaanites shifted and ceased to look like a crowd. Orderly rows formed before him. In the front, chariots. Then soldiers on horseback. And finally, men on foot, thousands upon thousands of them. The valley filled with them, and still more crossed the river.

The horses pulling Sisera's chariot reared up and then galloped from one end of the gathering to the other.

"He is rousing his men," Barak said. "They will begin their advance."

As he spoke, Sisera returned to the center and faced the mountain. His chariot charged forward, and his massive army followed.

Lappidoth's hand rose to grasp the hilt of his sword. "They are coming."

Silent, Barak continued to watch the scene below through eyes narrowed to mere slits.

Deborah exchanged a glance with her husband. His face had gone pale.

The Canaanite foot soldiers on either side ran forward but had no chance of keeping up with horse-drawn chariots. She watched as the first chariot reached the foot of the mountain and within moments they swarmed up the steep slope. A grumble sounded from those standing behind her.

And still Barak did not sound the attack.

"Watch," he said.

The lead chariot, the one in which Sisera rode, slowed. The others charged behind it, but when the horses began their ascent, their speed diminished. Before long, their orderly lines blurred as horses struggled to pull the heavy iron chariots uphill. They collided with one another. Deborah watched two of the beasts fall, and their chariots overturn. Chaos ensued as those behind crashed into the fallen.

She stole a look at Barak, who wore an expression of grim satisfaction. His words, uttered days ago before they began their own climb, returned to her.

"We hold the high ground," she said, and he jerked a nod.

Had he known this would happen? She believed he did.

Lappidoth pointed to the soldiers on either side of the wide trail. "They have reached the mound." When Barak made no answer, he said, "They will be upon our men in moments."

The trumpeter stepped forward, his hollow ram's horn clutched in both hands. He peered at Barak, his eyes begging to be given the sign.

"Come, Deborah." Lappidoth grasped her arm. "I must get you to safety."

"No!" Barak's head snapped in their direction. "She must stay."

"She is vulnerable," Lappidoth shouted. "In plain sight of the entire Canaanite army."

"And ours," the commander growled. "The men will be strengthened when they see Israel's judge standing above them."

Deborah placed a hand over her husband's. "Have no fear. Yahweh stands with me."

As the words crossed her tongue, a peace such as she had never known came over her. Not merely the lack of fear or tension but a deep, abiding peace. Yahweh's shalom.

She pressed his hand before releasing it. Straightening to her full height, she stood with her head high. Let the enemies of Yahweh look on her and tremble.

At last, Barak slid his sword from its scabbard.

"Sound the attack," he told the trumpeter.

The man put the horn to his lips. An earsplitting blast, long and penetrating, filled the air. A roar rose from the throats of ten thousand Israelites and reverberated across the mountain.

Barak held his weapon high above his head. "For Yahweh and Israel!"

He charged down the mountain. Deborah stood still as men swarmed past her, their battle cries numbing her ears. She caught sight of Uri, with Gersham at his side. In a flash they were gone, swallowed up in the mass.

Moments later the first sounds of war reached her. Clashing blades, guttural roars torn from men's throats, screams of pain—they combined into a discordant riot of human turmoil. The trumpeter sounded his horn once more and then sprinted after Barak, leaving Deborah and Lappidoth alone at the summit of Mount Tabor.

The battle raged up and down the side of the mountain. How long had she stood statue-like? Watching and listening. And praying. *Yahweh, save Your people. Save the men who have taken up arms for You.*

A wind whipped up in the valley and carried the sickly sweet smell of blood upward. Her stomach lurched whenever a gust blew in her direction.

Lappidoth stayed by her side, sword gripped in his right hand, his expression somber. "It is hard to tell Canaanite from Israelite."

Deborah allowed a humorous smile. "Ours are the ones who are winning."

It was true. Everywhere she looked, Israelite men swung axes and swords at their armored opponents. Some scooped up the weapons of their fallen enemies, while others wielded the shovels and winnowing forks they had brought from home.

A noise rose from the valley below, the blast from a trumpet. Not a ram's horn but one formed of metal that produced a high-pitched wail that pierced through the battle sounds. The result was immediate. The Canaanites still in the valley turned away. The ones battling on the mountain's side edged backward. Some abandoned their combat, whirled, and ran.

"They are retreating," Lappidoth said, relief plain in his voice. "It is over."

Deborah shook her head. "Did Yahweh not say He would utterly destroy our enemies? He will not leave any to attack Israel another day."

"But there are thousands still in the valley." Lappidoth turned toward her. "And hundreds of chariots."

She watched the retreating army swarm westward through the valley. The first of them reached the river and splashed into it without slowing. A mighty blast of wind whipped up the mountainside, so strong she had to plant her feet or be blown to the ground.

"Deborah, look."

From the western tree line, men swarmed into the valley. "Who is that?"

"I do not—"

Before he could finish the sentence, the two armies clashed. As she watched the newcomers fight, she saw not spears and chariots but axes and shovels and slings propelling rocks.

She grabbed Lappidoth's arm and squeezed hard in her excitement. "They are ours. They are Israelites."

"Barak must have sent a company around behind the Canaanites to cut off their retreat." A look of respect settled on his features. "He is truly a wise strategist."

They watched as the fresh Israelite men battled the weary Canaanites. They drove them back across the river as the main part of Barak's army advanced from the mountain. The enemy was trapped. It seemed only minutes before not a single Canaanite soldier stood upright. All the while the wind increased. Deborah and Lappidoth clung to each other, pressing forward against the force to keep their footing. Something about that wind seemed unreal. Divine, even. Where had she read about a Yahweh-sent wind?

When the answer came to her, she gasped. Yahweh sent a powerful wind when the Hebrew people raced to escape the Egyptians who sought to capture them and return them to slavery. The wind had been so powerful it parted the Red Sea and dried the land so Yahweh's children could cross in safety. And then, when the Egyptians tried to cross—

"Look there!" Lappidoth pointed.

She followed the line of his finger and her jaw dangled. A great flood of water gushed from an unseen point, as if Yahweh had emptied the Sea of Galilee into the Kishon River. A watery wall crashed westward, pushed before the mighty wind. Seeing it, the Israelites in the valley began to run toward Mount Tabor, and she held her breath until the last man set foot upon the sloping ground mere moments before the water overtook them. The wave hit the fallen Canaanites with such force that every chariot was washed away along with the slain soldiers.

A victory shout rose from thousands of Israelites who watched Yahweh's vengeance upon their enemies from the safety of the mountain.

Men returned to the camp, some weary and dragging their weapons, others still shouting in triumph, but all praising Yahweh. Deborah scanned each face as they passed. Finally she caught sight of one of the leaders and ran to intercept him.

"Where is Barak?" she asked, begging him silently not to speak the words she feared to hear.

"He has not returned?"

She shook her head. "I have not seen him since he sounded the attack."

Another joined them. "I saw him. When Sisera saw his cause fail, he ran away—the coward." A fierce pride settled on the man's features. "Not so our commander. Barak pursued the chariots. Just before the wave hit, I saw him charge after Sisera." He gestured toward the northeast. "In that direction."

"Deborah!"

With a nod of thanks, she turned to see Lappidoth beckoning to her. As she watched, Uri and Gersham stumbled toward him. Gersham carried someone slung across his shoulder, and with Uri's help, laid him gently on the ground.

Her heart in her throat, Deborah ran to them and looked down upon Tyrek's lifeless body. Blood covered him, his clothing soaked around an ugly wound in his chest.

"The archers led the attack," Uri said, his voice deep with sorrow. "He fell in the first wave."

Tyrek's body blurred behind a rush of tears. When she last saw him, he had been proud of his newfound skill and full of plans for his future. Ophira's face rose in her mind. How would she break the news to his sister?

"Abba?"

She looked up to see Gersham collapse. Uri threw his arms around Gersham's waist, stumbling beneath his weight, and Lappidoth rushed to his other side. Together they laid him on the ground.

Uri threw himself to his knees beside his father. "Abba, what is it?"

Deborah knelt at Gersham's other side. Blood covered him as well. She had assumed it to be Tyrek's, whom Gersham had carried. But now she saw thick red liquid flowing from a gash in his side. His breath wheezed, his chest shuddering with each breath. Looking up, she exchanged a sorrowful glance with Lappidoth.

"No." Uri leaned over until his face was inches above his father's. "Do not die," he shouted, his voice tight. "You cannot."

A weak laugh rumbled in Gersham's chest. "Watch me, boy."

Deborah sat back on her heels and whispered a prayer beneath her breath. She wasn't sure whether her prayer was for the father or the son.

A tear dripped from Uri's eyes onto Gersham's cheek, and he brushed it away with his fingers. Gersham's eyes fluttered open, and he lifted a hand. Uri grasped it in both of his, squeezing.

With effort, the dying man turned his head toward Deborah. "Will Yahweh turn His back on me"—he gasped a shuddering breath—"as I did...on Him?"

Uri lifted eyes full of agony to her, waiting for her answer.

"Torah teaches that Yahweh said to our father Moses, 'I am merciful and gracious, long-suffering, and abundant in goodness and truth; keeping mercy unto the thousandth generation, forgiving iniquity and transgression and sin.'" She forced a smile for his benefit. "We are far from the thousandth generation. Yahweh will not abandon you when you rest with your ancestors."

His eyes fluttered closed. "When I rest...with my Lilah."

"Abba, no," Uri said in an urgent whisper. "Elias and Zeb need you. I need you."

"Uri..." His body convulsed with a racking cough, cutting off his words. When the spasm passed, blood trickled from his mouth. He tried again to speak. "Proud of you," he finally managed.

Deborah watched Uri's face as tears streamed down his cheeks. Before her she saw only a grieving son, watching his abba's life slip away.

"Abba, listen to me." He rose up again to hover over Gersham. "You cannot die. Do you hear me?"

But Gersham was beyond hearing. His features went slack, and his hand slipped from Uri's grasp.

Deborah lifted her gaze to Lappidoth, her heart so full of anguish she could not utter a single word, while Uri collapsed, sobbing, across his abba's breathless chest.

CHAPTER TWENTY-EIGHT

Jael stood beneath the great oak, straining her eyes toward the mountains that lay beyond the plain to the south and west. Would Heber return today? More than a week had passed since he left her in the plain of Zaanannim to join King Jabin's army in Harosheth Haggoyim. Only once had she asked how long he would be away. She lifted a hand to brush her cheek, where the bruise he had given in answer still ached at night. After that she had not dared to ask again.

Seeing nothing in the distance, she picked up the milk jug and ducked inside their tent. If fortune smiled on her, she would have more days of solitude in this quiet plain. Still, she must be prepared for her husband's return. If he arrived to find no stew simmering over the fire and the wineskins empty, he would be angry. She had learned in the early days of her marriage to do everything she could to please her husband.

Leaving the milk inside the tent, Jael returned to the tree. She stretched the goatskin on the ground and picked up the sharp flint wedge she used to scrape the hair from the hide. Bent over her task, she applied the tool with practiced movements. When this hide had been cured and dried, it would be used to patch a hole in the tent, hopefully long before the rains fell again.

A shout reached her. Stiffening, she jerked her head toward the mountains again, and her gaze fell on a distant figure running in her direction. Her task forgotten, she jumped to her feet. Heber had returned. She dashed to the firepit and tossed lumps of dried dung on the smoldering ash then raced inside to fetch a bowl of lentils. After scooping up a few onions and wilted radishes, she returned to the fire and tossed them into a pot of water she kept ready. She stirred the ashes, relieved when the dung caught, and slid the pot into the pit.

Another shout reached her. He was closer. Her heart thudded in her chest. He would be here before the stew began to boil.

But why was he running?

Watching his approach, she was struck by a realization. The man advancing toward her was not her husband. His legs pumped with agility, not Heber's stomping gait. As he neared, she judged he would stand a full head shorter than Heber's hulking frame.

Was he a thief? Should she be afraid? Perhaps, but she felt only relief. It did not matter that the stew was not ready to serve. She was safe from her husband's anger, at least for now.

She stood still, watching the man's approach. When he drew close enough to study his features, she knew him to be a stranger.

He stumbled the last few steps and fell to the ground, his chest heaving and his breath noisy.

"Are—you—Israelite?"

Though the question itself was not unusual, the intensity with which he asked it aroused her curiosity.

"I am Kenite," she answered.

"Then you must—give—shelter." He struggled to rise up on his knees and drew in great gulps of air. "I am Sisera."

She knew the name. "The commander of King Jabin's army."

He nodded.

"Has the war begun?" she asked.

"Begun and ended." He scrubbed his hands across his face. "The Israelites called upon their God to strike us down." A laugh rose from his lips, high-pitched and frantic. "I heard they were led by a woman. A woman!"

The woman teacher. Deborah. Jael's mind conjured an image of her, seated beneath her palm tree, speaking words that Jael's own father had once spoken.

She stepped toward Sisera. "My husband fought with you. Heber the Kenite. Is he alive?"

"Did you not hear me?" he shouted, his eyes wild. "No one is alive. Their God struck us, and I am the only one left." He sank back and covered his face with his hands. "The only one."

Heber was dead. Her thoughts spun. Yahweh, the Israelite God, had destroyed them all.

She was free.

"I must rest." Sisera's words slurred with exhaustion. "You must hide me. When I have slept, I will return to King Jabin. We will raise another army, and this time we will crush the Israelites."

Jael stood looking down at him. Her husband had served under this man, had died fighting with him. Did he deserve her help, her pity? She felt none.

"Come," she said. "Come into my tent and rest. I will hide you."

He allowed her to help him up and leaned heavily on her as they crossed the short distance to her tent. Inside, she led him to the sleeping mat.

Throwing himself on it, he said, "I am thirsty. Please bring me water to drink."

"Water for the commander of the king's army? Wait here, my lord."

After going to the crate where she kept her dishes, she withdrew a bowl, the only one left from her childhood home. Heber had broken the rest. This one had been glazed a glimmering purple, with a bright multicolored design painted on its side. She filled it with fresh, thick milk and brought it to Sisera.

"Drink this," she told him. "It will help you rest."

When he had drained the bowl, she covered him with Heber's blanket. He turned onto his side and relaxed beneath it.

"Stand in the doorway," he said in a voice already heavy with sleep. "If anyone comes, tell them no one is here."

She stood at the opening of her tent and scanned the surrounding plain, as he bade her to do. In only a few minutes, his breath fell into a deep, even pattern. She waited until she was sure a sound would not wake him before slipping outside.

Steam rose from the stewpot, which had just begun to boil. From a pile nearby, she picked up the heavy hammer Heber used to drive tent pegs into the ground. Taking it and an unused peg, she returned to the tent and crept softly to the mat. Once there, she sank to her knees. Sisera did not stir. His mouth hung open, his jaw slack in sleep.

She pitched her voice low. "You will not lead another army against the people of Yahweh."

Positioning the sharp end of the peg over Sisera's temple, she raised the hammer.

Jael sat beneath the oak, working on the skin with which she would patch her tent. Soon she would leave this place. Where would she go? To the Wilderness of Zin? Perhaps, but she did not think so. Deborah's words, words from Israel's Torah, spoken when she sought the teacher's wisdom, returned to her.

"The stranger that dwells with you shall be unto you as one born among you, and you shalt love him as yourself, for you were strangers in the land of Egypt. I am Yahweh, your Elohim."

Perhaps she would go to Ephraim, to Deborah's Palm.

A man she did not know approached, as she had known he would. This one was tall, even taller than her dead husband. His well-muscled arms spoke of strength, and the light in his eye of zeal.

"I am Barak son of Abinoam, of the tribe of Naphtali," he said. "I am looking for a man."

Setting aside the sharp wedge and the skin, Jael rose. "Come with me," she said. "I will show you the man you seek."

CHAPTER TWENTY-NINE

D eborah stood behind the worktable beside Sabra, watching her chop figs.

"That is good," she said, "but smaller pieces will blend more easily and cook more evenly. Let me show you."

She took the knife and reduced the moist pile into tiny morsels.

Sabra's lips twisted sideways. "I have been chopping figs since I could hold the knife."

"Then why have you not mastered the task?"

Though she tried to sound stern, Deborah could not hold back a teasing grin. Laughing, Sabra took the knife from her unresisting hand and picked up another fig.

Lappidoth stepped inside from the courtyard. Lifting her head, Deborah met his gaze. They exchanged a private smile. Since returning from Mount Tabor, their appreciation for one another had gained new depths. It took no effort at all for Deborah to conjure an image of him standing beside her, clutching his sword, ready to defend her at the cost of his own life if the need arose.

His gaze slid to their daughter. "Sabra, your betrothed has arrived."

The knife hit the worktable, immediately forgotten. She dashed toward the doorway, coming to an abrupt halt as Uri stepped inside holding a crate.

Deborah watched the young man's eyes light when he caught sight of Sabra. Her heart warmed. Gone was the arrogant Uri, deserted on the slopes of Mount Tabor. This one who traveled home with her and Lappidoth and the others stood taller, smiled often, and craved the words of Yahweh like a starving man craves a scrap of bread.

"I brought you a gift," he told Sabra, and thrust the crate toward her.

"Another gift?" Doda Yocheved's booming voice preceded her appearance from Sabra's bedchamber. She marched into the room, planted her hands on her hips, and aimed a scowl in Uri's direction. "If you keep bringing her gifts, you will have nothing left for her mattan."

Her gruff reprimand did not dim his smile in the least. "Go ahead," he told Sabra. "I want to know what you think."

Sabra carried the crate to the worktable, her eyes shining. Deborah saw straw filling the inside. Clay pots, if she were to make a guess. Judging by the pride on Uri's face, he had made them himself at the pottery wheel in Yosef's workshop.

Upon their return, Uri had gone straight to his brothers with the news of their abba's death. From there he had accompanied Deborah and Lappidoth to speak to Ophira. Deborah had sat silently, listening as he described how he and Tyrek had become friends on the northbound journey. When he spoke of

Tyrek's skill with the bow, of his pleasure in learning, and of the friendships he made among the archers, tears spilled down Ophira's face. Tears of sorrow, Deborah knew, but also of joy to know that her brother had finally found happiness.

When Deborah and Lappidoth returned home, Uri left to seek out Yosef and offer himself as an apprentice in Tyrek's place.

"Well?" Yocheved demanded, craning her neck to see inside the crate. "What has he brought this time?"

Sabra plunged a hand into the straw and drew out a small pot. She gave a delighted squeal. "It is for my cheese."

Wearing a proud smile, Uri nodded. "A dozen of them. See here, around the rim? A thin strip of cloth, such as you use to tie down the waxed cover, will fit right inside and will not slip."

He touched the pot in her hand, and his fingers brushed hers. Sabra's cheeks blushed pink at the contact.

"Yosef is sending some of my work to the market in Shiloh along with his and Reuben's," Uri announced. "He believes they will find buyers there."

Sabra clutched the little pot to her chest and turned shining eyes up to his. "They will. I know it."

"Deborah."

Deborah lifted her gaze from her daughter's face to her husband's. "Have you forgotten the time?" he asked.

Startled, she hurried to the window to check the position of the sun. "It is nearly the sixth hour."

"I have seen a steady stream of people climbing the hill to Deborah's Palm," Lappidoth told her. "Word has spread, and people are eager to hear your song."

Heat flooded her cheeks, as Sabra's had flushed moments before, though for a different reason. Today she would sit beneath her tree and sing the song Yahweh had given her, the one she and Barak sang together when he returned from Zaanannim dragging Sisera's body, wrapped in a blanket, behind him.

"Come, Wife." Lappidoth held out his hand.

She abandoned the half-chopped figs on the worktable and came to his side. Together they left the house, the others following.

"There is one you will not see today, though I am sure you will be pleased to hear it," he said as they walked.

She knew who he meant from the sour note in his voice. "Asif."

"The same. He paid me a visit this morning while I worked in the olive grove. He wanted to tell me how disappointed he is in me."

Surprised, she said, "In you?"

He nodded. "That I have not exercised sufficient control over my wife and forced her to stop pretending she speaks for Yahweh." He shook his head. "You know I have no taste for violence, but I confess I wanted to slap him for belittling my wife."

"I feel nothing but pity for Asif," she told him.

Then it was his turn to be surprised. "How so?"

"Asif's mind is small, and therefore his idea of Yahweh is small. If only he could have stood atop Mount Tabor and witnessed the power of Yahweh." She lifted a shoulder. "But he does not want to see. And for that, I pity him."

They reached the hill then. Holding tightly to his hand, Deborah began the ascent. Her thoughts strayed to another slope they climbed together, and she saw from the slight curve of his lips that he, too, remembered.

When they reached the top, he pressed her hand once and then released it. He, Uri, Sabra, and Doda Yocheved joined those seated on the hilltop.

Deborah's gaze swept the faces before her, many of them familiar. Tivon sat beside Adena. Nearby she spied Dara, Chaim, and Laban. Ophira was there, her pregnancy no longer hidden, with Reuben and Yosef. Next to them were Rachel, Seth, and Shira alongside Anna and Levi with young Tobias between them.

Besides her friends, she saw many from the village who had never before come for her teaching, and even more she had never seen. The crowd stretched far ahead of her, filling the clearing and even down the western side of the hill. As Lappidoth said, word had spread, and the people of Israel were hungry to hear of Yahweh's victory.

She rested her hand on the trunk of her palm tree. *Blessed are You, Yahweh, King of the universe, who fills my heart with joy and my mouth with songs of praise.*

Lifting her arms to the heavens, she took a breath and began to sing.

THE SONG OF DEBORAH

On that day Deborah and Barak son of Abinoam
sang this song:
"Israel's leaders took charge,
and the people gladly followed.
Praise the Lord!

"Listen, you kings!
Pay attention, you mighty rulers!
For I will sing to the Lord.
I will make music to the Lord, the God of Israel.

"Lord, when you set out from Seir
and marched across the fields of Edom,
the earth trembled,
and the cloudy skies poured down rain.
The mountains quaked in the presence of the Lord,
the God of Mount Sinai—
in the presence of the Lord,
the God of Israel.

"In the days of Shamgar son of Anath,
and in the days of Jael,

people avoided the main roads,
and travelers stayed on winding pathways.
There were few people left in the villages of Israel—
until Deborah arose as a mother for Israel.
When Israel chose new gods,
war erupted at the city gates.
Yet not a shield or spear could be seen
among forty thousand warriors in Israel!
My heart is with the commanders of Israel,
with those who volunteered for war.
Praise the LORD!

"Consider this, you who ride on fine donkeys,
you who sit on fancy saddle blankets,
and you who walk along the road.
Listen to the village musicians
gathered at the watering holes.
They recount the righteous victories of the LORD
and the victories of his villagers in Israel.
Then the people of the LORD
marched down to the city gates.

"Wake up, Deborah, wake up!
Wake up, wake up, and sing a song!
Arise, Barak!
Lead your captives away, son of Abinoam!

"Down from Tabor marched the few against the nobles.
The people of the LORD marched down
against mighty warriors.
They came down from Ephraim—
a land that once belonged to the Amalekites;
they followed you, Benjamin, with your troops.
From Makir the commanders marched down;
from Zebulun came those who carry a commander's staff.
The princes of Issachar were with Deborah and Barak.
They followed Barak, rushing into the valley.
But in the tribe of Reuben
there was great indecision.
Why did you sit at home among the sheepfolds—
to hear the shepherds whistle for their flocks?
Yes, in the tribe of Reuben
there was great indecision.
Gilead remained east of the Jordan.
And why did Dan stay home?
Asher sat unmoved at the seashore,
remaining in his harbors.
But Zebulun risked his life,
as did Naphtali, on the heights of the battlefield.

"The kings of Canaan came and fought,
at Taanach near Megiddo's springs,
but they carried off no silver treasures.
The stars fought from heaven.

The stars in their orbits fought against Sisera.
The Kishon River swept them away—
that ancient torrent, the Kishon.
March on with courage, my soul!
Then the horses' hooves hammered the ground,
the galloping, galloping of Sisera's mighty steeds.
'Let the people of Meroz be cursed,' said
the angel of the LORD.
'Let them be utterly cursed,
because they did not come to help the LORD—
to help the LORD against the mighty warriors.'

"Most blessed among women is Jael,
the wife of Heber the Kenite.
May she be blessed above all women who live in tents.
Sisera asked for water,
and she gave him milk.
In a bowl fit for nobles,
she brought him yogurt.
Then with her left hand she reached for a tent peg,
and with her right hand for the workman's hammer.
She struck Sisera with the hammer, crushing his head.
With a shattering blow, she pierced his temples.
He sank, he fell,
he lay still at her feet.
And where he sank,
there he died.

"From the window Sisera's mother looked out.
Through the window she watched for his return, saying,
'Why is his chariot so long in coming?
Why don't we hear the sound of chariot wheels?'

"Her wise women answer,
and she repeats these words to herself:
'They must be dividing the captured plunder—
with a woman or two for every man.
There will be colorful robes for Sisera,
and colorful, embroidered robes for me.
Yes, the plunder will include
colorful robes embroidered on both sides.'

"LORD, may all your enemies die like Sisera!
But may those who love you rise like the sun in all its power!"

Then there was peace in the land for forty years.
—Judges 5 (NLT)

Letter from

THE AUTHOR

Dear Reader,

My research for this story took me to places I have never visited in person, but now they're on my bucket list. Deborah was an amazing woman. She lived in the twelfth century BCE, and yet she learned to read and write, which was unusual for a woman of that time. She knew Torah better than many, and she heard from God! How did that happen? Scripture doesn't tell us, so the novelist in me had to make a few assumptions. I guess we won't know all the details for sure until we step into eternity and get to talk to her face-to-face.

This book takes place in the earliest time period I've ever written, so I had to revise many of my previous assumptions. During Deborah's lifetime there was no king of Israel, and never had been. There were no synagogues, or a temple. For their pilgrimage festivals, all Israelite men were required to journey to Shiloh, in Ephraim, which was more or less centrally located in the promised land. Imagine the crowd! People put up tents all around the tabernacle, where Yahweh dwelled in the ark of the covenant along with the stone tablets He had given to Moses and a jar of manna. Many years ago, I took my young son to a Boy Scout jamboree, where we pitched a pup tent amid hundreds of others. As I wrote Deborah's story, I imagined that sight magnified by thousands.

Reading well-researched and well-written biblical fiction makes the Bible come alive for me. Writing it is even better. It has been a pleasure and a joy to write Deborah's story. I hope you come to love her, as I have.

Signed,
Virginia Smith

BOOK GROUP QUESTIONS

1. In what ways do you identify with Deborah in *The Woman Warrior*?
2. Have you heard God's voice, as Deborah did? What did He say? How did you respond?
3. Which character in this story resonated the most with you? Why?
4. Have you experienced conflict with your spouse or a close friend because of God's direction for you or for that person? How did you resolve the conflict?
5. Biblical fiction, such as *The Woman Warrior,* is often based in scripture and historical fact, but many of the details are drawn from the author's imagination. Does this deepen your connection with biblical truths? Why or why not?

A SCHOLAR'S VIEW OF THE
BOOK OF JUDGES

When the Hebrews traveled out of Egypt, they came to Sinai to discover a God who spoke through fire and smoke on the mountain peak. Their victories in battle established that Yahweh would deliver them as they journeyed through the desert toward the Promised Land, the lush green fields along the Jordan River in the land called Canaan. However, once they crossed the Jordan, their needs changed. Crops had to be planted and animals raised. Would this YHWH also provide for them here? From a distance many centuries later, the answer appears obvious. It was not clear as the nomads became settlers.

The land was divided twelve ways, with Asher and Naphtali in the north and Simeon in the south. In between, the rest of the tribes fell into place with Rueben, Gad, and Manasseh bordering the Jordan River on the west.

Barely had the Hebrews settled into the land when problems arose. Other tribes posed a threat to their existence. Moabites, Hittites, Hivites, Perizzites, Midianites, Amorites, and Philistines stood ready to destroy them.

Out of this division would arise the twelve judges who would guide the Hebrews during these perilous times. Some would be people of significant faith; others would not. The stage was set for a drama more demanding and dramatic than any television series.

We can draw a parallel in our time when young people go off to summer camp. Singing "Kumbaya" by a campfire, teenagers make a commitment to be faithful and enduring Christians. And then they go home, back to the temptations and complexities of everyday life. Will their devout intentions professed around the evening fire carry them through the struggles of daily living? Will their faith in God still be there when they are faced with the unexpected problems of adulthood? The same God will be there. But will their faith in Him still remain?

Israel as a nation was challenged by the same questions. What happened?

The answer is found in the book of Judges. Judges 2 through 3:6 paints a picture of how the inspired leaders faced the challenges of Israel's enemies. These verses tell us that the warring tribes were left in place by God as a challenge to the faith of the Israelites. Each generation had to make its own commitment to the Covenant and could not depend on the faith of their parents behind them to carry them through. They would be tested by the attackers to determine if they would remain faithful to the Covenant that had been made and established at Sinai. The judges would lead them through this struggle.

Because we can read the entire book of Judges in twenty minutes, it is easy to conclude that the individual judges came one after the other. But in fact, the time of the Judges can be measured in centuries and was composed of a cycle that repeated again and again. We might think of it like the face of a clock that rotates from A to B to C to D. The letters give us a mnemonic way to remember what happened to the Israelites during these cycles.

A = Apostasy

As the Hebrews stand at the edge of the Jordan, Joshua warns them what will happen if they forget their heritage. If they intermarry with the natives and are unfaithful, the Lord God will not keep His hand upon them. The remnants of the tribe left in the land will be a scourge to the Israelites. They have been warned!

The Israelites start in a position of loyalty to YHWH, but are soon challenged by the religions of the indigenous people. They've heard from their neighbors that the land and animals respond to the Baals, the gods of fertility. And if the crops don't grow nor the animals reproduce, the tribes are in great danger. The Israelites begin looking to these gods of fertility and nature to see if they can bring better results. Slowly, the tribes drift into idolatry, to apostasy.

B = Battered

The Israelites begin to assimilate and become like their idolatrous neighbors. They start to lose the lessons that Moses taught them to have no other gods but Jehovah, YHWH. The Israelites begin to forget their identity as they are battered by the outsiders.

Their infidelity brings disaster. Attacks from warring tribes threaten their existence. The gods of the soil appear to be stronger and are responsible for bringing defeat to Israel, now

running scared in the face of the fierce strength of their enemies. They are broken.

C = Cry

Judgment comes upon them because of their failure, and
the Hebrews realize their error. They begin to remember again
the singular nature of their God, and they know that infidelity
and arrogance have brought disaster upon the House of Israel.
They cry out to God for His intervention.

D = Deliverance

With their backs to the wall, after crying out for help, a
judge appears, bringing renewal through the divine hand.
Previously an ordinary person, the judge arises out of the midst
of the tribes and leads the people back to victory. Because the
Israelites have returned to YHWH, a new day dawns among the
tribes. They are delivered from the hands of their enemies.

So in order to understand the judges, all we need to do is
remember our A-B-C-D's. As a loose confederacy, the Hebrews
had no head of state or king to guide them. Consequently, the
role of the judge was to provide the leadership needed to hold
them together in their struggle. The twelve judges made the
difference. They were: Othniel, Ehud, Shamgar, Deborah,
Gideon, Tola, Jair, Jephthah, Ibzah, Elon, Abdon, and Samson.
Only six were given a prominent position in the book of Judges.
Deborah was the only woman.

Beginning in the twelfth century BC, Deborah led for sixty
years. For twenty of those years, she struggled with the hard-
ships imposed by the Canaanite war followed by forty years of
peace. With a name meaning bee or honeybee, Deborah was

particularly renowned for her moral character and loved by the people as she fulfilled the role of prophet, national leader, and military commander.

Jabin, the king of Canaan, had his capital in Hazor and continually oppressed the Israelites. In order to stop this threat, Deborah called on Barak to raise up an army of ten thousand troops. Opposing him, the warrior Sisera commanded Jabin's army. Deborah prophesied that YHWH would deliver Sisera into Barak's hands. Of course, this is exactly what happened, ending with Jael driving a tent pin through Sisera's temple.

The Song of Deborah celebrates victory by applauding the work of two women: Deborah the prophetess and Jael the warrior. The people of Israel were saved by YHWH to return to their faith in the one God who stood over them.

Fiction Author
VIRGINIA SMITH

Bestselling author Virginia Smith's first novel was published in 2006. Since then, she's written more than fifty books that have collected a satisfying number of accolades and awards, including two Holt Medallion Awards of Merit. An avid reader with eclectic tastes in fiction, Ginny writes in a variety of styles, from light-hearted relationship stories to breath-snatching suspense. She and her husband live in the bluegrass state of Kentucky (where the grass is green, not blue) with a feisty Maltese named Max.

Nonfiction Author
ROBERT L. WISE, Ph.D.

The Rev. Robert L. Wise, Ph.D., is the author of thirty-five books and numerous articles published in English, Spanish, Dutch, Chinese, Japanese, and German. On the internet he weekly publishes *Miracles Never Cease* and monthly presents live interviews on YouTube with people who have experienced divine interventions.

*Read on for a sneak peek of another exciting story in the
Extraordinary Women of the Bible series!*

THE GOD WHO SEES: HAGAR'S STORY

BY MELANIE DOBSON

The sun bowed before the jeweled throne of her father and then lashed its tail across Hagar's dusty toes. Morning had just begun, and already the heat was upon the caravan as they marched toward the city gate, her face beaded with sweat, her lips parched.

How would she survive a journey through the wilderness with no shade for her shaven head?

Not that she cared much about her survival. She was an outcast now. A girl with no mother and a father—the ruler over Egypt—who seemed to have forgotten that she belonged to him. She was supposed to marry a pharaoh one day, rule at his side as the Royal Wife, but she had no future as a slave.

On the street ahead, a ragged group of slaves prodded flocks of sheep and goats through a crowd who'd gathered to ensure their departure. Egyptians parted like the banks of a riverbed, giving Abram's company plenty of space to flow rapidly through the street and out the gates that had kept the Hebrew men and women dammed inside. No one in Egypt wanted to hinder the departure of the strangers who'd inflicted a plague on their land.

Wanderers, that's what the Hebrews were called. A small band of thieves could easily overtake their group in the wilderness, Hagar thought, but neither Abram with his wooden scepter in hand nor his wife, who walked regally at his side, seemed worried about desert thieves as they guided the clumsy retinue to the city gate. Instead they held their heads high, and Sarai's long hair, the color of sand, draped like elegant curtains over her shoulders, her linen tunic hiding her skin. Nothing like the shorn heads of Egyptian women and sheer garments worn by the royal court.

The wicked vizier's eyes were fixed on Hagar's father, and many of those crowding the street also watched Pharaoh instead of the Hebrews, his face stoic even as a panel of slaves stood behind him, fanning his skin with feathers. So different from the Hebrew couple. To Abram and Sarai, it seemed, Pharaoh had faded into the backdrop of his palace, one stone among thousands in his kingdom.

Hagar longed to feel a breeze over her skin. To be bathing with the other princesses in the cool waters channeled into a separate palace built for Pharaoh's lesser wives. To be holding her mother's hand again, laughing together under a covering of palms as she'd done for most of her twelve years.

Instead, she was being sent into the desert, far from everything she'd ever known. The only piece of Egypt going with her, a glazed doll, hung around her waist with a papyrus rope, hidden between the folds of her tunic.

She gently rubbed the shabti doll that knocked against her side with every step. The desert might be riddled with thieves, but she was a thief as well. Instead of a pearl or diamond, she'd stolen this one piece before a guard tore her away from the palace, the stone doll meant to accompany her mother to the afterlife. The only thing Hagar had left to remember.

A woman wailed in the distance. Had she lost someone she loved to the Hebrew plague? Hagar didn't understand all that had happened since the last full moon, but many in their kingdom, including her father, were covered in black sores. Several of his attendants had been ushered into the afterlife from this wretched disease.

Her father would do anything to placate this curse, sacrifice anyone or anything in his kingdom to wipe out the scourge on their nation, but the temple gods hadn't listened to his pleas. Sending Sarai away was supposed to appease Abram's God.

What god was more powerful than Pharaoh?

Slaves continued cooling her father's speckled skin with ostrich feather fans on the balcony, flitting away any bits of dust that might contaminate his wounds. Pharaoh was god in flesh to their nation, but now a greater god, the God of Abram, had inflicted him, and all their people were scared.

Sitting beside Pharaoh, as prim and regal as a peacock, was the Royal Wife, a slight woman named Chione who wore a sheer dress and a collar made of bright turquoise beads, her shaved head covered in a black wig and the prized golden cobra coiled around her lofty crown. Powdered galena, mixed with oil, lined her dark eyes to diffuse the glare of sunlight. Even though Hagar was far from the throne, she knew the woman's skin had been slathered with olive oil to ward off the plague, her gown doused in perfume.

The Royal Wife might be small in stature, weak in might, but Hagar knew well the strength of her intelligence surpassed any man in Egypt. Chione was both cunning and greatly admired by Pharaoh and those women who lived outside the royal court. The women inside the palace were terrified of her.

While she didn't want anyone to be afraid of her, Hagar still dreamed of being like Chione. In the three months since her mother had died, she'd longed for respect. Admiration, even. To be remembered as a princess instead of being cast aside.

Hagar stared at her father on his throne, a desperate plea rising inside her. Why wouldn't he look at her? His oldest daughter. One of many children that, just months ago, he would visit in the harem courtyard.

He once brought her gifts and asked questions and doted on her as if she were prized among his flock. *Treasure* is what he'd called her. Like gold. Turquoise. Lapis lazuli. Carnelian. All brilliant gems tucked into pockets of earth.

But she was no longer treasured. Nor was she welcome in the palace or in all of Egypt. At the age of twelve, she was being expelled from his kingdom as a slave.

If only he'd look her way. Just a nod of his head, the simplest of motion, to say goodbye. But instead of seeing his daughter, Pharaoh's eyes were fastened on the woman who led their parade.

Sarai wore no makeup like the Egyptian women. No lead to line her eyes or jewels to decorate her neck. Even without the gems and cosmetics, she was the most beautiful woman Hagar had ever seen. Pharaoh could have almost anything he wanted in Egypt—their gods rarely refused him—but they hadn't given him Sarai. It seemed to Hagar, in the whispering she'd heard, that Pharaoh wanted nothing else except this woman, and Chione was jealous, as she had once been of Hagar's mother.

The priests and priestesses stepped out of the temple to hasten the unwelcomed guests and their newly acquired bounty on their journey back into the wilderness. If the band of travelers didn't leave this morning, there would be an uprising, and Hagar would be caught in the middle.

A man on her left wore the head of a falcon for Horus, the eye of the sun. A priestess wore the head of a cow to demonstrate that the kindness of the goddess Hathor overflowed like milk.

Egypt was Hagar's home, the only home she had ever known, but lately she hadn't found much kindness in Egypt. Her back still ached from the lashings she'd received before Abram arrived, and her stomach churned from hunger. Even though she was in the midst of a crowd, she had never felt more alone.

A young man, barely fifteen, slipped onto the balcony between Pharaoh and the Royal Wife. Amun's chest was bare, like Pharaoh's, a skirt hanging short above his sandals. Chione reached for his hand and clung to it as if she could oversee the life of her son as she did his father. Amun didn't need a defender, but his mother would do anything necessary to secure for him the jewel-encrusted throne.

Unlike Pharaoh, Amun quickly located Hagar in the crowd and lifted his free hand to wave. He'd wanted to rescue her, promised her as much, but her half brother had no power over a god. Even though Amun begged for Hagar to stay, Pharaoh had still sent her away with five other slaves to care for Abram and Sarai and a host of Egyptian animals they were taking with them.

A baby goat cried out below her elbow, its voice raw, and Hagar placed her hand on the kid's head to comfort it until it quieted. This small animal was probably more valuable in her father's eyes than his daughter. It might grow into a ram, worshiped as the god of Khnum. Definitely more valuable than a girl who would never be a god.

When Hagar raised her hand to wipe the sweat from her shaved head, the kid nudged her side. She ran her fingers again over a tuft of gray fur on its back.

"Where's your mother?" she asked as if the animal might conjure a voice beyond its cry to answer.

The creature pressed its body into her as if Hagar could protect it from the wicked rays of sun. She scanned the herds in the clouds of dust but saw no nanny looking for its offspring. Every kid, she thought, should have a mother. Even though she was twelve, she still longed for hers.

"I'll take care of you," Hagar whispered before lifting the animal.

The kid melted into her chest, and she didn't care what those in the crowd thought of her carrying the goat like a child. Or, at least, she tried not to care. Egypt had already rejected her and her mother.

The only people she had to please now were her new master and mistress. If she served them well, Amun had told her, she would have food and a safe place to rest.

Right now, she wished for food more than rest. No one had remembered to feed her this morning.

"Hagar!" someone called.

Her heart leaped. Perhaps her father had finally changed his mind and sent an aide to fetch her. She could return to the royal court.

"Kiki," the voice called again, and she turned. Only one person called her *monkey*.

Amun pressed through the crowd toward her. He'd always hated the name Hagar. Forsaken was what it meant. Abandoned. Forgotten. Left alone.

Stranger.

If only one could change her name. Her future.

"What is it?" she asked when Amun stepped into the caravan beside her. Perhaps she could stay in the palace after all, far from the vizier who had hated her and her *mata*.

"Why are you carrying a goat?" His voice sounded much lighter than the worry that tugged down his handsome face.

"She needed someone to carry her," she replied, a tentative smile on her lips.

"Kiki—"

"Did you ask him again?" She held her breath, waiting for the answer that could change everything. If only she could return to the palace and be protected again by Pharaoh, as she'd been as a little girl, or by Khnum, the goat-god who was supposed to protect them all.

Amun nodded slowly, but no smile tugged the edges of his mouth as he accompanied her through the sea of people.

"And he has refused...."

"If you stay here..." Amun's words were swept away in the voices around them, the bleating of animals and the stomping of feet. "He fears for his life, I think."

"I am a child," she said. "No man need fear me."

Amun smiled again, the warmth of a half brother who had known her since birth. "You are no longer a child."

She brushed her hand over the goat's fur. "I still feel like one."

"Jamila will be with you in the wilderness," he said, pointing to one of the slaves ahead, an Egyptian woman a few years older than Hagar.

"I don't know Jamila." Nor did she know how to befriend a fellow slave.

"She'll still watch over you, and you'll have Medu too."

Amun shouted Medu's name, and the youth glanced back. He was older than Hagar as well, about Amun's age, his shaven head glistening like hers as he led a herd of goats toward the gates.

"Take care of my sister," Amun instructed as if he were Pharaoh himself instead of a fifteen-year-old boy trying to find his way.

Medu nodded at them before he goaded an animal back into the fold, directing the small flock toward the gate.

"Medu was a temple slave," Amun explained. "But he seems to prefer caring for animals outside the temple walls. He is ready to leave Egypt."

It might feel like an escape, freedom even, for those like Medu and Jamila, who'd spent a lifetime enslaved, but the leaving was agony for her.

As they neared the gate splitting the city wall, two watchmen heaved on ropes to open the lattice. Wood and metal grated against each other as if warning the wanderers about what lay on the other side.

"Kiki." Amun said her name quietly now as he escorted her to the gate. "I have something to tell you."

She pulled the goat closer to her chest. Her heart couldn't handle another blow, not when she felt as if it were already splayed on the ground. "I don't think I can bear to hear it."

"Here." He held out a cloth bundle in his hands, filled with grapes and a corner of cheese, then set it on top of the goat's back. "This is for you."

She thanked him for his kindness.

"I'll miss you," he said, with the saddest of smiles. "But one day, I will find you."

She watched the sunlight flicker in green eyes that usually embraced the fullness of laughter. "You can't find a wanderer."

"Perhaps you can wander back to Egypt."

"You are a dreamer, my brother," she said. "When you are Pharaoh, you won't want me here."

The caravan stopped as light flooded through the open gate. Hagar bumped into the hind end of a sheep, but Amun didn't laugh at her.

She placed the kid goat on the ground and held his gift to her heart before embracing Amun, not wanting to ever let him ago. But when the crowd started rustling around them, he stepped away.

"I will find you," he said again as if making a solemn vow.

How she wished she could take him with her. He would never be able to locate her in the vast wilderness, no matter how many accompanied him on his search.

Abram and Sarai, their hands entwined, proceeded through the opening between the mud-brick walls. Unlike Hagar, they were ready to leave the strength and safety of Egypt.

She turned to wish Amun a final goodbye, but he had already disappeared into the crowd.

People crowded around her, pushing her forward, but the little goat didn't leave her side. Hagar picked up the animal again and squinted toward the empty space between the walls, trying to see the void on the other side. She'd visited the wide river before, even traveled down it once during her tenth year, but she'd never been beyond it.

What was it like in the wilderness? And how would she survive in this new world without Amun?

Three boats waited on the riverbank while several crocodiles basked in the sunlight on the far bank. Egyptian men manned each skiff, waiting to row them across the Nile, to leave them with the awaiting band of crocodiles while several slaves would take the flocks north to cross at the shallow delta.

Once Abram and his company left Egypt, they would be banished for life.

As the caravan moved toward the river, the city gate slammed with a thunder that echoed across the river valley. Then she heard another roar. A rumble of applause and cheers.

The plague was leaving Egypt, and Hagar had no choice.

She had to follow it into the wilderness.